BREAKING THE SILENCE

Human Rights Violations Based on Sexual Orientation

AMNESTY
INTERNATIONAL
UNITED KINGDOM

ISBN 1873328125
First published 1997

Amnesty International United Kingdom
99-119 Rosebery Avenue
LONDON EC1R 4RE

This report is based on documentary material researched by the International Secretariat of Amnesty International. Some material contained in this book was previously published in the United States and Canada in February 1994 by Amnesty International USA. The text has been substantially revised and updated, and contains additional introductory material.

Grateful thanks are due for assistance with this book to Ignacio Saiz and Adrian Sanchez of the Research Department of Amnesty International, to Stonewall and Gay Times for help with pictures and information, to Simon Russell of the Refugee Legal Unit and to Shirley Armstrong, producer of the Amnesty International Netherlands video, Breaking the Silence.

Printed by Ennisfield Print and Design

BREAKING THE SILENCE

Human Rights Violations Based on Sexual Orientation

The picture on the cover of "Breaking the Silence" is from a painting by Salvador Salazar, a gay artist from Mexico City, to commemorate the killing of a Mexican transvestite, "Vanessa", shot dead on the streets of Tuxtla Gutiérrez in southern Mexico in 1993, reportedly by a member of the Chiapas State Judicial Police. At least 12 local transvestites were the victims of "death squad" murders between 1990 and 1995 (see pages 14 - 16 of this book). The artist carried his painting on a protest demonstration in Chiapas against the killings in 1995.

"Vanessa" - Neftalí Ruiz Ramírez - was a transvestite performer, a human rights defender, and the Vice President of the Tuxtla Gutiérrez Gay and Transvestite Group. She organised denunciations and protests against the murders, and against the wrongful imprisonment of three men who had been tortured by the police into making false confessions to the killings.

Investigations into the murders were blocked throughout by officials, and marred by torture, corruption, death threats to witnesses, cover-ups and forced confessions. There was evidence that the actual perpetrators of the crimes acted with the tolerance and complicity of the Mexican authorities. Four of the police officials allegedly involved in the killings have since been promoted. To date nobody has been successfully prosecuted for any of the murders.

CONTENTS

INTRODUCTION

BREAKING THE SILENCE:
SEXUAL MINORITIES AT RISK

In countries all over the world, individuals are being targeted for imprisonment, torture and even murder, simply on the grounds of their sexual orientation. Gay men, lesbians, transvestites, transsexuals any person who doesn't adhere to the dictates of what passes for "normal" sexuality may be subject to such persecution at the hands of private individuals or government agents. Abuses may take subtle forms such as everyday hostility, harassment or neglect. In such cases, antipathetic authorities may refuse to protect the basic rights of gays and lesbians, leaving them vulnerable to exploitation, sexual attack, public or domestic violence and even murder, all without recourse to the law. In other instances, governments are themselves the perpetrators of abuses: unfair trials, imprisonment, ill-treatment (including false "medical cures"), torture (including rape), and execution are among the violations recorded by Amnesty International.

No international protection for sexual minorities
Much of the impetus for the development of international human rights law as it exists today emerged in reaction to the atrocities committed during the Second World War. Like Jews, gypsies, and the disabled, lesbians and gay men were targeted for extermination by the Nazis. As many as one hundred thousand men were identified as homosexuals and transported to concentration camps. Wearing the pink triangle (since adopted as the international symbol of the gay rights movement), these men were among the millions shot, hung, gassed, worked or starved to death in the camps. Several thousand lesbians met the same fate. Identified not as homosexuals but as "anti-social elements," lesbians wore the black triangle and lived, laboured, starved and died alongside vagrants and petty

criminals who had received the same classification.

Despite this clear indication of their particular vulnerability to human rights abuses, gay men and lesbians were not specifically included in the framework for international human rights protection when the United Nations drew up the Universal Declaration of Human Rights after the war's end. Systematic discrimination against some vulnerable groups has been addressed in subsequent documents such as the *International Convention on the Elimination of All Forms of Racial Discrimination and the International Convention on the Elimination of All Forms of Discrimination Against Women*. These documents have provided an important framework for combating violations against women and ethnic minorities, yet there has been little recognition in the international community that gay men and lesbians require – and deserve – similar protections. Although case studies demonstrate that a woman in prison may be singled out for rape because she is a lesbian, although a man may suffer police violence because he is known to be homosexual or believed to carry the AIDS virus, human rights violations on the grounds of sexual identity are not yet expressly forbidden by any international law.

At the World Conference on Human Rights in Vienna, Amnesty International voiced its concern for the rights of sexual minorities in its proposals, specifying provisions for "vulnerable groups which require greater attention within the human rights programme including children, indigenous peoples, people with disabilities, religious, sexual, ethnic and linguistic minorities, and those afflicted by HIV and AIDS." This proposal (not adopted as part of the final document created by the Vienna Conference) signals Amnesty International's belief that gay men and lesbians around the world remain at risk.

Fighting the battle for protection under existing laws

In theory, gay men and lesbians should enjoy the protection of the general human rights treaties, such as the *International Bill of Human Rights, the International Convention on Civil and Political Rights,* and the *International Convention on Economic, Social and Cultural Rights* which are intended to secure "all rights for all people". In some countries, sexual minorities have won legal protection for their rights on the basis of existing laws. The *European Convention for the Protection of Human Rights and Fundamental Freedoms* has already provided a whole series of important decisions in favour of gay and lesbian rights. In 1988, Senator David Norris, a longtime campaigner for homosexual rights, successfully argued that the Irish law which allowed the prosecution of consenting adults for homosexual acts was constitutionally invalid and in violation of the *European Convention*. The law in question was consequently struck from the books, as were similar laws in Northern Ireland and Cyprus following similar decisions.

At the same time, other countries are putting laws that specifically protect gays and lesbians into effect. In the United States, ten states now explicitly prohibit discrimination on the grounds of sexual orientation. And in May of 1996 the Republic of South Africa became the first nation to incorporate sexual orientation into the anti-discrimination provisions of its constitution.

Gays and lesbians remain at risk

Given the enhanced public awareness of gay and lesbian rights issues, given that some battles are being won in the courts, why is it that general human rights protections so often fail to shield gay men and lesbians from serious abuses?

First, many homosexuals who have been the victims of repression fail to report the violence against them. They may fear that their sexual orientation may be made public as a result of speaking out, thereby laying them open to further violence and social ostracism. They may have a well-founded lack of trust in the authorities which should protect them, such as the police or social services. They may feel that their complaints will not be taken seriously or, worse, that their protest will bring down the wrath of those who harmed them, making them the target for serious reprisals. In many cultures, lesbians and gay men are so socially, culturally, and economically marginalized that they lack the barest resources to defend themselves, call attention to their ill-treatment, or mobilize public opinion in their support. Lesbians may face double discrimination, because of their sex as well as their sexual orientation. The silence that grows out of such marginalisation and fear makes it difficult for concerned human rights agencies to monitor abuses or take action on the part of victims.

Next, discriminatory treatment of gays and lesbians is often "masked," concealed behind bogus legal pretexts. In such cases, the victims may be officially charged with any number of offenses in order to hide the true reasons behind their detention, imprisonment, torture or execution. "Vagrancy," "hooliganism," "child molesting," and "unruly behaviour" are only a few examples of charges used to bring sexual minorities under the power of the state. Once in custody, they may be subject to extreme and unusual forms of abuse including false "medical treatment" to "cure" them of their "illness".

Because of age-old, deeply-held social and religious taboos, some governments are reluctant or unwilling to admit to the presence of gays and lesbians in their midst – let alone take steps to defend their human rights! They may see the issue of protections for gay rights as a foreign concept, forced on them by the domineering West. They may deny government involvement in abuses, turning a blind eye to violations and maintaining that, since private individuals are at fault, they can do nothing about them. Or, on the contrary, they may stridently defend their right to punish what they see as a criminal offence. As the appendix of this book shows, homosexuality, particularly sodomy between men, is still criminalized in many countries today. Same-sex relationships may be deemed "deviant", "unnatural", "immoral", or "against God's will". They may be seen as a threat to "family values" or to the fabric of society at large. The terror of AIDS and HIV infection has lent ammunition to many who hold such views – and has led to a new category of human rights violation: those targeting individuals because of their real or perceived HIV/AIDS status. Governments who promote, fail to challenge, or attempt to disguise the persecution of gays and lesbians create a climate where abuses proliferate in secrecy beyond the reach of international human rights protections.

Bringing gay and lesbian human rights violations into the open

As part of its mission to defend the human rights of all people,

Amnesty International works to identify, expose, and combat human rights abuses which specifically target individuals because of their sexual orientation. Amnesty International believes that sexual orientation is a fundamental dimension of human identity and as such should be treated as a basic human right. Educating the public and garnering support for victims are among Amnesty International's chief aims. Part One of this report is a grim survey of cases collected from countries all over the world. The accounts tell of men and women harassed, detained, tortured, tried, imprisoned and even executed because of their sexual orientation or their activities on behalf of sexual minorities. Part Two offers a more positive outlook. It is a survey of some of the excellent work being done by gay and lesbian groups to promote human rights and fight abuses. Part Three of this report details Amnesty International's own role in protecting the rights of gay men and lesbians, while Part Four spells out Amnesty International's recommendations to governments to ensure the protection of these rights.

PART 1

HUMAN RIGHTS VIOLATIONS TARGETING GAY MEN AND LESBIANS

Governments violate the human rights of their citizens. Unfair trials, torture (including rape), cruel and degrading practices and even murder are used by authorities to intimidate and control. Amnesty International has evidence of governments in all regions of the world directing human rights abuse specifically at homosexuals. This book is a survey of some of Amnesty International's evidence of the widespread violations of civil, political, social and economic rights that sexual minorities face around the world. It is not meant to be an exhaustive analysis.

The violations faced by lesbians and gay men range from subtle discrimination and everyday hostility to imprisonment, torture, and execution by agents of government. Lesbians and gay men around the world face violations of their human rights in common with other citizens, but they also suffer specific abuses geared to their real or perceived homosexuality, such as practices aimed at forcibly "changing" their sexual orientation. The stigmatised position of gay men and lesbians around the world contributes to their experiences of ill-treatment at the hands of authorities.

Extrajudicial Executions and "Disappearances"
Extrajudicial executions are deliberate and unlawful killings by, or with the consent of, the state. Such killings are prohibited under international law, but are reported by Amnesty International each year in scores of countries. They are often perpetrated by shadowy "death squads" acting as covert arms of the state, with official approval. The authorities claim to be unable to control such killers and refuse to accept responsibility for ending their abuses and bringing those responsible to justice. Their targets include political

© Gordon Rainsford, Gay Times

Participants in Pride Festival, London 1996

opponents of the government in power, members of racial or ethnic minorities, or others considered "undesirables". Death squads are often present in countries that are undergoing extreme civil unrest. But they may also emerge outside any context of conflict when police or security forces join with private interests to eliminate those they consider to be troublesome or otherwise dispensable, and therefore appropriate scapegoats for national ills.

When lesbians and gay men are the targets for such operations, they are particularly vulnerable. There is little or no social or political support available to defend them, nor to expose, denounce or stop the abuses. The consequences of speaking out against such persecution can be fatal.

An enforced "disappearance" takes place when there is reason to believe that a person has been taken into custody by agents of the state, and the authorities deny that the victim is in custody, thus concealing their whereabouts or fate. This human rights crime has been regularly reported each year by Amnesty International in dozens of countries. It is a violation of many different rights, as prisoners vanish into secret cells without even an acknowledgement that they have been detained, that they are alive, that they will ever be seen again. Among those targeted in some countries are lesbians and gay men. Human rights activists have been obliged to prove wrong, against enormous odds, the jailers' refrain to the prisoner that "no one knows you are here" or that "no one knows you're even alive".

In Mexico, between 1991 and 1994, twelve gay men were killed in the city of Tuxtla Gutiérrez in the State of Chiapas. Nine were shot, one was stabbed to death and two were beaten to death, as part of a pattern of violence directed against the gay community in this area. Many of the victims in this economically marginalised sector were transvestite sex workers and gay activists. Local gay and lesbian groups also drew attention to another four possible cases of similar killings but the authorities refused to link these with the other twelve. One of those slain was Neftali Ruiz Ramirez, Vice President of the Tuxtla Gutiérrez Gay and Transvestite Group. Ramirez was a

© Amnesty International

Neftali Ruiz Ramirez in demonstration against gay killings in Chiapas with other members of the Circulo Cultural Gay, Mexico, October 1992.

transvestite performer, who had taken part in protests against the killings. He was shot dead, reportedly by a member of the State Judicial Police. The investigations into the Tuxtla Gutiérrez killings were blocked by the authorities, and marred by evidence of torture, cover up and forced confessions. To date nobody has been successfully prosecuted for any of the killings.

Three men who had been initially rounded up for some of the Tuxtla Gutiérrez murders, and had been tortured and beaten into making false confessions, were all released, one after his eight- year sentence for murder was overturned on appeal. There was evidence that the actual perpetrators of the crimes acted with the tolerance and complicity of the Mexican authorities. The systematic failure to bring those involved to justice has granted virtual impunity to the perpetrators. Indeed, four of the police officials allegedly involved in the killings have since been promoted. The investigations failed to carry out thorough, impartial or prompt inquiries and were riddled with irregularities, hampered by death threats to witnesses and to journalists reporting developments. Special Prosecutor Jorge Gamboa Borraz, appointed in April 1994 to investigate the killings,

Photo ©Adrian Sanchez

Protest against the Tuxtla Gutiérrez murders, 1994

resigned in June 1994 due to what he described as "a lack of cooperation from the authorities". In 1994 the Department of Human Rights of the Archdiocese of Mexico reported that over thirty gay men had been killed between 1991 and 1994, possibly with state involvement.[1]

Because of the acute difficulties that any lesbians and gay men experience in trying to claim their rights under the law, and the reluctance of state officials to protect these rights, abuses committed against them are particularly difficult to monitor and punish. It is difficult to measure the level of abuse. The crimes tend to be under-reported, the perpetrators go unpunished. The victims have been largely "invisible".

In Colombia, with one of the highest murder rates in the world, hundreds of death squad killings of so-called "social undesirables" or "disposables" have taken place in urban areas. It is only recently that these killings have come fully on to the domestic human rights agenda.

"For gays in Colombia, there is no rule of law. The only program the government has for people like me is a program to kill us... There were a group of fifteen of us working the streets that were HIV positive and that the police knew about... From January to May of this year (1993) five of us had been killed. Picked up in police cars, shot and dumped."

Luis Alberto, male prostitute

What Colombians have termed limpieza social "social clean-up operations" target the urban poor, gay men, transvestites, male and female prostitutes, street children, vagrants and petty criminals. Victims of these "death squads" are gunned down in the streets at night or seized and driven away in unmarked cars. Their bodies, which are rarely identified, often bear signs of torture. In most cases the killers remain unidentified, although there is often evidence of the direct involvement of the security forces, including off-duty members of the National Police. Although there is no evidence of any central command structure for such killings, the systematic failure of the government of Colombia to take the steps which are in its power to bring them to an end effectively makes it complicit in these murders. According to the now-disbanded Colombian gay organisation Grupo De Ambiente, between 1986 and 1990 some 328 gay men were murdered in the city of Medellín alone. The Washington Office on Latin America has reported regular "runs" by the Bogotá Police in which male prostitutes were forced to run down a hill while local police fired on them.[2]

In Brazil, local gay groups claim "death squad" killings have led to the assassination of hundreds of members of sexual minorities over the past fifteen years.

On the evening of 14 March 1993, Renildo José dos Santos, a bisexual member of the local council, who had publicly acknowledged his sexuality on a radio programme, was violently abducted from his home in Coqueiro Sêco, in Alagoas State in North East Brazil, by a group of unidentified heavily armed men. Relatives of the councillor who witnessed the abduction believe that some of the men were plain clothes police officers. Dos Santos' headless body was found two days later in an area of waste ground. It bore the marks of torture.

Colombian soldier searching a bus at an army checkpoint, 1987

17

Renildo José dos Santos had repeatedly denounced the death threats against him which he claimed he had been receiving since 1989 from the local mayor and the mayor's father, also a political leader. He also accused a local police officer of making an attempt on his life. According to his written testimony in September 1991, he had reported the death threats to a local judge, but he claimed that no steps had been taken to ensure his physical safety. On 27 November 1991, he was shot and wounded three times, allegedly by a local police officer whom he named in his testimony. He attributed the death threats and the attempt against his life to political differences with the mayor and the mayor's father, and to publicity about his bisexuality. He claimed the local police had not conducted a proper investigation into the attempt against his life. The local police officer who he reported as having shot him had not been

© Jornal de Alagoas

Renildo José dos Santos

suspended from duty pending the outcome of the investigation.

In January 1993, the local council of Coqueiro Sêco set up a parliamentary commission of inquiry to investigate the conduct of Councillor dos Santos under accusations that he had committed acts "incompatible with Parliamentary decorum" – i.e. homosexual acts.

As a result of the inquiry, he was stripped of his local council seat, but was subsequently reinstated, pending a judicial appeal. On 25 February 1993, several local human rights organisations wrote to the Alagoas State Secretary for Public Security denouncing the death threats and the alleged involvement of military police officers in the attempts on the councillor's life. However, to Amnesty International's knowledge, no protection was granted to ensure his safety. In a statement to the newspaper Jornal de Alagoas a few days before his assassination, Councillor dos Santos had reiterated his denunciations of death threats and of discrimination against him, and attributed the smear campaign to his public acknowledgment of his bisexuality. He said that he was frightened and desperate and that he feared a new attempt on his life or an abduction.[3]

Those who come to the aid of homosexual human rights victims are sometimes targeted themselves. After the Dos Santos murder, Reinaldo Cabral, a correspondent for a Rio de Janeiro newspaper Jornal do Brasil, wrote an article denouncing police violence and the threats of continued violence against two of dos Santos' relatives. In the early hours of the morning of 8 April 1993 two unknown men entered the front garden of Cabral's home. While one of them held a gun, the other poured petrol over Cabral's car and set it on fire before fleeing.[4]

On 13 June 1994 two human advisers to the Brazilian Workers Party, lawyer Reinaldo Guedes Miranda, and poet Hermó genes Da Silva Almeida Filho, were shot dead in their car. The two men had received threatening phone calls apparently relating to their activities on behalf of back people and homosexuals. Their killer was a police informer.[5]

Arbitrary Killings by Armed Opposition Groups
Amnesty International works against kidnapping, torture and arbitrary killings by armed opposition groups. In a number of countries, such human rights abuses are directed against gay men and lesbians.

In Peru in 1994, the gay rights group Movimiento Homosexual de Lima, who also work against police abuses of lesbians and gay men, reported that gays were being assassinated by the Tupac Amaro Revolutionary Movement (MRTA), an armed insurgency group.[6]

Torture and Ill-Treatment

Torture is illegal under international human rights law, and most national legal codes. The 1984 *International Convention Against Torture* defines torture as the act by which severe physical or mental pain or suffering is intentionally inflicted on a detainee, by or with the acquiescence of a public official, to punish, obtain information, intimidate, humiliate or coerce.

Each year Amnesty International carries reports of torture from over half of the member states of the United Nations. Torture and ill-treatment are used by many governments around the world to suppress dissents, intimidate political activists and threaten certain sectors of the population. Torture is also used in non-political settings when it is targeted at particular groups in the community. Lesbians and gay men in the custody of government officials are particularly vulnerable to torture and ill-treatment.

International laws against torture oblige governments not only to prevent torture, but to investigate, prosecute and punish the torturer and compensate the victim. The state bears responsibility for its agents if they participate or acquiesce in the torture of anyone, including lesbians or gay men in their custody. The failure of a government to prosecute its agents in such circumstances breaches its obligations under international human rights law.

In some countries, homosexual activists are targeted as "examples," in attempts to control their public identities and community activism. In other places gay people living relatively quiet and private lives may fall victim to this type of government abuse. Torture and ill-treatment are sometimes used to force "confessions" of homosexuality, or to elicit the names and addresses of other lesbians and gay men. Lesbians and gay men who face such abuses are doubly victimized, as societal discrimination prevents them from seeking the legal, religious, social, or psychiatric support services available to other victims. The fact that such abuse is often not reported, renders the wounds even more difficult to heal.

In 1996 in Romania sexual acts between consenting gay men or lesbians were still punishable by one to five years imprisonment under Article 200 paragraph 1 of the Romanian penal code. Gay men were routinely targeted for ill-treatment and torture.[7]

"I was sentenced to five years because of my homosexuality. It is terrible in jail. We were treated as if we were the most serious criminals. Everyone was treated better than homosexuals. When I was arrested the police beat me and tortured me. In jail the torture continued, physically and emotionally. It was terrible. Even the neighbours inform the police. The police know everything about everyone."

Ioan, Romanian ex-detainee

Doru Marian Beldie, nineteen, was arrested in Bucharest on 16 June 1992, and charged with having sex with a minor. Beldie was reportedly beaten with truncheons on the palms of his hands and soles of his feet by police in the 17th District Police Station for several hours in order to force him to sign a confession. He was sentenced to four and a half years in prison under Article 200, paragraphs 1 and 2 of the Romanian criminal code for homosexual relations with a minor. In prison he was allegedly raped repeatedly by other prisoners.

Marcel Brosca, twenty, a Romanian student, was arrested in March 1992 in Tecuci. He was beaten and ill-treated by police officers until he signed a confession that he had performed oral sex with a minor. According to the report received by Amnesty International, at the time of his arrest he was commuting by train to his native village from Galati where he studied. He overslept and woke up in Tecuci. As there was no train back that same evening he went to sleep in the station waiting room. He was reportedly awakened by four policemen accompanied by a seventeen-year-old boy. Pointing to Marcel the policemen asked the boy if this was the man for whom they had been searching. The boy responded affirmatively. Marcel Brosca was reportedly beaten for three or four hours after being detained by the police; he was then pulled by the hair, the sides and back of his head were beaten against the table and the wall until blood poured over his face, his arms were twisted, and he was beaten on the soles of his feet with truncheons. He was convicted under Article 200 paragraph 1 and 2 of the Romanian criminal code and sentenced to five years in prison.[8]

In Venezuela, the Law of Vagrants and Crooks (*Ley Sobre Vagos y Maleantes*), 1956, allows detention for up to five years for those deemed a threat to society by the police. Often these are people against whom there is no evidence of a punishable crime that could stand up in court. In practice the law's definitions are so vague that almost anyone can be detained simply on suspicion of being a "vagrant" or "crook" or having a previous criminal record. It is almost exclusively targeted against the poorer members of society suggesting discrimination on the basis of social origin.

The law has been used by the police to imprison homosexuals accused of prostitution. In May 1994 Amnesty International representatives visited the El Dorado Rehabilitation Centre, the prison where a number of people detained under this legislation are sent. Prison conditions were described as appalling. Facilities were grossly inadequate, with foul water, insufficient food and inadequate medical care. Amnesty International interviewed two men, prisoners of conscience, held under the Act solely because of their sexual orientation: Pedro Luis Peña Arévalo ("Colina") who works as a transvestite prostitute in Maracaibo, and José Luis Zapata ("Liliana") from Caracas. Pedro Peña Arévalo was arrested in May 1993 and sentenced to thirty months imprisonment under this law. In prison he was reportedly shot in the leg and buttock by a member of the security forces, allegedly because of his sexual orientation. In Barcelona Prison he was also reportedly beaten with *peinillas* (sabres) by prison guards and subjected to repeated harassment by other prison staff and members of the National Guard in Casa Amarilla, another prison.

José Luis Zapata, who had already been detained for four years from 1986 under this law, was again arrested in 1993 and held in a number of prisons where he was harassed by both prisoners and guards, he believes because of his sexual orientation. In his own words, "They beat me for being who I am."

In Peru, Amnesty International has been concerned about police raids on gay bars and discotheques in the capital, and the harassment, arbitrary arrest, ill-treatment and other forms of persecution of people working in defence of lesbian and gay rights in Peru, including the Lima Homosexual Movement, *Movimiento Homosexual de Lima,* and the Human Rights Association' *Asociacion Pro Derechos Humanos* (APRODEH). In three raids on Lima's downtown district over six hundred people, including gays, lesbians and transsexuals, were arrested, shoved into police trucks, held in police stations without charge, and reportedly subjected to verbal abuse, humiliation and attempts to solicit bribes. The raids appeared to have been targeted at persons because of their real or perceived homosexuality rather than any search for any individuals and minors in the bars and discotheques without documents, as claimed by the police.[9]

> *"In 1994 in Lima a very violent raid was carried out in the capital where about seventy-five lesbian women were beaten up and ill treated by the police. Prostitutes get a very rough time in jail. But the treatment of lesbians was even worse. Lesbians were beaten up because, however degrading prostitution can be, it is still regarded as normal behaviour, whereas lesbianism is seen as too threatening to the status quo."*
>
> Anonymous Peruvian witness

Allegations of ill-treatment of homosexuals by police in the United Kingdom have been made to Amnesty International by people who believe the abuse was directed at them because of their homosexual identity and/or their racial or ethnic group affiliation. Some of these complainants have been awarded civil damages.[10]

© Amnesty International.

Pedro Peña Arévalo and José Luis Zapata

© Nicky Warden

Amnesty International members collecting signatures to a petition to the Mayor of New York about New York Police Department attacks on gay men. London 1996

Complaints of ill-treatment by police officers in the United States have also been received over the years by Amnesty International. In 1996 the organisation published a report on police brutality and excessive force in the New York City Police Department (NYPD), which highlighted a number of cases of alleged ill-treatment of people because of their sexual orientation.

Greg Maro was harassed in Times Square in 1990 by a group of teenagers who he said had thrown a bottle at him because he was gay. When he sought assistance from an NYPD police officer, he was allegedly hit, handcuffed, dragged across the ground and verbally abused by the officer, who, according to Maro, said that he was a "fag-basher" himself. Maro's complaint against the officer to the Civilian Complaints Board was ruled "unsubstantiated". The officer who was reportedly involved in the incident had been the subject of three prior misconduct complaints and had participated in an incident in which he was severely criticised by a district attorney. In 1994 he was reported to be involved in the training of new officers.

Christopher Henelly is an activist in the organisation Act Up which campaigns for homosexual equality and for action on AIDS. He was allegedly beaten up by police while taking part in an Act Up demonstration for lesbian and gay rights outside a Manhattan police station in February 1991, protesting against the alleged ill-treatment of another Act Up member the previous week. Henelly spent five days in hospital with cerebral concussion, partial loss of hearing and blurred vision, and reportedly suffered from seizures as a result of his injuries. The case of assault against the police that the New York Police Department had brought against him was dismissed by a judge when he saw the video film of the incident. It showed the police charging into the crowd of demonstrators, without provocation, one police officer being seen turning Henelly's head round and taking a two-handed swing with his club on the spot on his head where Henelly's arrest photograph showed a bruise.[11]

In Iran, lesbianism and male homosexual acts short of consummation are punishable by lashes. Flogging is a punishment

Public flogging in Iran

25

of prisoners that Amnesty International considers cruel, inhuman and degrading.

In Saudi Arabi, individuals convicted of homosexual behaviour generally face a custodial sentence and flogging. In October 1996, twenty-four Filipino migrant workers were arrested for homosexual behaviour. They were reported to have been sentenced to two hundred lashes each. The sentences were to be administered in four punishment sessions and to be followed by the men's deportation from the country. The individuals were reportedly not engaging in sexual intercourse.[12]

In Turkey, homosexuality is not officially illegal, but police regularly raid the homes of gay men and lesbians and make arrests. Transvestites in Istanbul are concentrated in Cihangir, a part of Beyoğlu District, and have frequently complained about harassment by the police. Once detained, Turkish gay men and lesbians, particularly gay rights activists, may be subjected to harassment, intimidation and ill-treatment. In recent years, homosexuals and transvestites, in Istanbul in particular, have begun to address these problems publicly. Some have spoken nationally and internationally on behalf of those marginalised in Turkish society.[13]

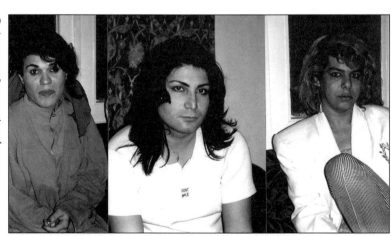

Three Turkish transvestites, Ilhami Kaya, Yasar Pinarbas and Seyfettin Turan, were arrested in Cihangir, Beyo lu District, Istanbul and reportedly ill-treated by the Turkish police, November 1995

Ali, a gay man who had just fled Turkey, addressed attendees of the Dutch Lesbian and Gay Pride Day in the Netherlands in June 1994:

> *"I have stayed in police stations for three days. They hit me and they tortured me. Four days ago my best friend was killed in the police station in Ankara. Because I am homosexual I have been sexually abused and raped many times and in unimaginable ways while being held at police stations. It is wrong that you are not taken to hospital straight away. That is partly because you are a homosexual. If you go there during the day everyone can see that the police have beaten you. That's why it often happens that people die in front of their friends or lovers. I have suffered a lot simply because I am a homosexual."*

On the night of 10 August 1991, the houses of several transvestites in Istanbul were raided by the local police. Six people were detained, including Ramazan (Demet) Demir, a member of the Istanbul Human Rights Association and a gay rights activist. On his release, six days later, Demir alleged that he had been severely beaten with a length of a rubber-covered steel hose by the Chief of Police at Beyg lu Police Station. He obtained a medical report from the Forensic Medical Institute certifying that he had injuries consistent with his allegations. After publicly protesting his torture, he was again detained and finally charged with "insulting the memory of Mustafa Kemal Atatürk" after he pointed out to the arresting officers that homosexuality was not proscribed by the laws which had been introduced by Atatürk.[14]

In November 1994 Amnesty International reported the arrest and beating of three members of the Gay Albania Society, *Shoqata Gay Albania*, Albania's first gay organisation. The three men were reportedly beaten severely in Tirana District 1 Police Station. One was admitted to hospital unconscious, with multiple fractures on his leg. Another was also injured by beatings. During their detention police reportedly accused them of belonging to an illegal organisation and demanded the names of members.[15]

Rape and Sexual Abuse

Rape and other forms of sexual assault in custody, including the insertion of objects into the orifices of the body, have been described by the UN's Special Rapporteur on Torture as:

> *"...a particularly ignominious violation of the inherent dignity and right to physical integrity of the human being, they accordingly constituted an act of torture."*

In some countries, rape and sexual abuse by government officials is a common method of torture inflicted on female detainees. This method of torture is also sometimes used against men. Rape is a physical assault and injury, as well as an assault on the victim's sexual identity and thus their mental and emotional well-being.

Interrogators and other government officials may use rape and sexual abuse to force "confessions" of homosexuality, or use these rapes as "proof" that the detainee is a gay man or a lesbian, or else to attempt to force lesbians to "change" their sexual orientation.

Homosexuals who have been raped may be afraid to report such abuses because the very act of admitting to them could be seen,

Police make arrests during a raid on transvestite quarter of Istanbul

contradictorily, to confirm the suspicions of the detainee's homosexuality. Further compounding the violation, domestic judicial and legislative remedies for the victims of such abuse may in practice be unavailable to lesbians and gay men who have been raped in detention because of their fears of ostracism, or loss of family support.

Among numbers of transvestites arbitrarily arrested in San José, Costa Rica in early 1993, at least seven were reportedly detained by police agents in April 1993. They were held for several hours and subjected to degrading treatment. One of these men, Manuel Horacio Guevara Albornoz, was reportedly arrested wearing women's clothes. He was taken to the radio patrol unit, where policemen reportedly mocked and fondled him. He was re-arrested in May, taken to the same radio patrol unit, made to strip, and subjected to further mockery. José Enrique Vargas Gonzalez, who was also arrested in May 1993 by two policemen, was driven to the ruins of a house, and reportedly forced at gunpoint to have oral sex with one of the officers. Investigations into these cases were carried out by the Costa Rican Ministry of the Interior.[16]

Forced "Medical Treatment" to Change Sexual Orientation
The behaviour and lifestyles of gay men and lesbians have often been classified as psychological disorders resulting in forced hospital treatment. Whereas male homosexual behaviour is more likely to be punished in law, research has shown that lesbians are more likely to be subjected to psychiatric "treatment" on the grounds that their sexuality is considered pathological rather than criminal. This may include mind-altering medicines, electro-convulsive therapy and other ill-treatment. In some countries, lesbians and gay men in custody have been subjected to forced "medical" treatment to change their sexual orientation. This kind of abuse included electric shock and other forms of "aversion therapy", or the use of psychotropic drugs.

In 1982, Amnesty International condemned "medical" treatment carried out on people in detention against their will for the purpose of attempting to alter their sexual orientation.

There were widespread reports of this kind of ill-treatment in the former Soviet Union, and in China in the 1970s and 1980s where the *New York Times* reported the application of painful electric shocks and induced vomiting to discourage erotic thoughts in homosexuals.

In Romania at the time of Nicolae Ceausescu, imprisoned homosexuals were given electro-convulsive therapy, according to the Romanian gay rights group, ACCEPT.

Asylum-Seekers

Amnesty International's work on behalf of asylum-seekers stems from its goal to protect people from arbitrary detention, torture, killing and "disappearance". The organisation has worked over the years to prevent the enforced return (*refoulement*) by governments of gay men and lesbians who flee persecution in their homeland because of their sexual orientation. The organisation also opposes barriers in the asylum arrangements of states that discriminate against anyone solely because of their sexual orientation.

© Stonewall

Stonewall demonstration for the rights of gay asylum seekers.
London 1996

Under the *Geneva Convention*, refugee is defined as someone who, "owing to a well-founded fear of being persecuted for reasons of race, religion, nationality, membership of a particular social group or political opinion" is unwilling or unable to return to his or her former country of origin or habitual residence.

In recent years a growing number of countries have accepted as grounds for de facto refugee status, applications from gay and lesbian asylum-seekers who cite their persecution for sexual orientation under "membership of a particular social group" as spelled out in the Convention. These include the Netherlands, Denmark, Ireland, Norway, Finland, Australia, Germany, New Zealand, the United States and Canada. In each of these countries important precedent setting cases have been fought and won by gay asylum-seekers.

On 4 April 1992 in Canada, Jorge Alberto Inaudi, a gay man from Argentina, successfully won his case for asylum before Canada's Immigration and Refugee Board on grounds that, as a member of a particular social group, he would face persecution for his sexual orientation if he were to be returned to his country of origin.

In 1984 the Wiesbaden Federal Administrative Court in the Federal Republic of Germany ruled that gay men in Iran can be perceived as political opponents of the regime because of the peculiarly theological nature of the Iranian State, and offered asylum to a gay man from Iran on grounds of the extreme political situation that he would face if returned to his country of origin.

On 12 March 1994, Mr Toboso-Alfonso, a gay man from Cuba, successfully appealed to the United States Supreme Court against the refusal of his asylum application as a member of a "particular social group" with a well-founded fear of persecution because of his sexuality. The United States Court of Appeal found in his favour. When gay Congressman Barney Frank asked Janet Reno, the US Attorney-General, if this decision amounted to a precedent in US law, she replied in the affirmative.

In the United Kingdom, case law on whether homosexuals can constitute "a particular social group" for refugee status appears to be in some disarray. 1991 the Immigration Appeals Tribunal found that gay men did not constitute a particular social group in the case of

Mr Golchin (7623), a gay Iranian asylum seeker. Mr Golchin was granted Exceptional Leave to Remain in Britain, it being accepted that his situation, if he were to be returned to Iran would be "intolerable". However his argument about belonging to a particular and persecuted social group was not accepted. In contrast, in the case of Mr Vraciu, a gay man from Romania, the Immigration Appeal Tribunal finding (11559) was that homosexuals in Romania do constitute a social group as defined under the Convention.

In the United Kingdom a gay male model from the Soviet Union successfully applied for asylum and was granted full refugee status in 1991. Mr Jelab (7571), a Syrian national, won his case for asylum on the grounds that homosexuals in Arab countries were at particular risk of persecution from the police and government.

Laws Criminalising Homosexuality
In an appendix to this book there is a "rough guide" to the state of criminalisation of homosexual acts under the world's penal codes. This has been compiled from various sources of information available at the time of writing. The trend internationally in recent years has been strongly towards decriminalisation, backed up by successful challenges brought by regional and international human rights bodies.

However, many countries still have laws that enable officials to imprison gay men and lesbians simply for giving expression to their sexual identity, either through public advocacy of homosexual equality, or through their sexual relations in private. These laws are sometimes said to protect society from "immorality", "unnatural carnal sex", "acts against the order of nature", or even from "bourgeois perversion". Under such laws it becomes illegal to be a gay man or a lesbian.

Sex between people of the same gender is punishable by a maximum sentence of execution in a number of Islamic and/or Asian countries, and by long sentences or lashes in a number of African countries. Laws penalising homosexuality exist in many Commonwealth countries. In India Section 377 of the Penal Code bans "carnal intercourse against the order of nature". Gay activists say the law leads to harassment of gay men in India. In Nigeria male homosexual acts are punishable with up to fourteen years in prison.

Lesbians and gay men have historically been persecuted and oppressed by means of laws that criminalise sexual behaviour between consenting adults of the same sex, even when such behaviour occurs in private. The language of these laws varies with regard to the specific acts which are proscribed: the common effect is to stigmatise lesbians and gay men as criminals. While these laws are not always used by authorities to imprison lesbians and gay men, in many cases their existence provides the context for discrimination and violence against gay men and lesbians.

The years since the fall of the Berlin Wall in 1989 have seen increased freedom and visibility for gay men and lesbians. In most of the countries of the former Soviet Union and other former Warsaw Pact countries, anti-gay laws have been repealed and organisations fighting for gay rights have been recognised officially. In May 1993 Russia decriminalised consensual sex between males which, prior to then, had been an offence punishable by up to five years' imprisonment. Other former Soviet republics have also decriminalised similar laws, Ukraine in 1991, Estonia in 1992, Lithuania in 1993, and Belarus in 1994. In Latvia, the Minister of Justice told Amnesty International that all "persons who had been punished for homosexuality were immediately released from punishment after the adoption of the [new] legislation" in 1992. In other countries that have amended their laws, some individuals detained under anti-homosexual laws may nevertheless remain in captivity.

A few former Soviet republics have retained their sodomy laws. In Uzbekistan, the new criminal code, which entered into force in 1995, retains as a criminal offence consenting homosexual activity between men. According to the Justice Minister of Uzbekistan in 1992, a small number of men had been convicted since independence under a similar article in the previous criminal code. Amnesty International expressed concern about the continuing existence of such laws in other former Soviet republics such as Georgia (where there were moves in 1994 towards decriminalisation), Kazakhstan and Kyrgyzstan.[17]

Albania decriminalised homosexual behaviour between

consenting adults in June 1995. In a letter to Amnesty International the gay rights organisation Shoqata Gay Albania said that Albanian politicians who took the decision to end the law punishing gay sex with ten years of imprisonment had been strongly influenced by letters and messages received from abroad following the arrests and beatings of gay men and campaigners for human rights in Albania in 1994.[18]

© Gordon Rainsford

Hugo Greenhalgh, Ralph Wilde and Will Parry

In 1992 in the United Kingdom the House of Keys on the Isle of Man repealed local laws that had made consensual sex between adult men punishable with sentences from two years to life imprisonment.[19]

In 1993, Ireland (following the European Court of Human Rights action by Senator David Norris) repealed its laws criminalising consensual sex between adult men, and shortly afterwards enacted anti-discrimination legislation.[20]

Age of consent laws define the age at which national laws permit sexual activity. The benchmark of eighteen years of age is often taken for adulthood, but there is no universal age of consent for sexual activity whether homosexual or heterosexual – it varies from state to state. Many countries, including the United Kingdom, have a higher age of consent for homosexual sexual acts than for heterosexual activity. Amnesty International recognises governments have the right to determine the age of consent, but is concerned that age of consent laws could be used in an unjustifiably discriminatory way to imprison lesbians and gay men. The organisation would consider cases for adoption as prisoners of conscience where a consenting party would be considered a sexually mature adult in law as regards heterosexual relations, but a minor as regards homosexual acts.

In 1994 a major national campaign was organised in the United Kingdom, led by the gay rights movement Stonewall to lower the age of consent for homosexual acts (then twenty-one) to the age for heterosexual sex (sixteen). Many human rights organisations in the UK , including Amnesty International, lobbied Parliament calling for equalisation of the age of consent. In the event Parliament narrowly decided to lower the age of consent for homosexual acts to eighteen.[21]

In 1996 two young gay men from the United Kingdom, Chris Morris (sixteen) and Euan Sutherland (seventeen), petitioned the European Court of Human Rights claiming that the UK legislation was discriminatory.

In Nicaragua, Amnesty International is concerned that Article 204 of the Penal Code (Amended 1992), which aims to penalise gay men and lesbians, could result in the prosecution and imprisonment of prisoners of conscience for expressing their homosexual identity or for advocating gay rights. The Article, upheld by the Nicaraguan Supreme Court in 1994, provides that: "Anyone who induces, promotes, propagandises or practices in scandalous form sexual intercourse between persons of the same sex commits the crime of sodomy and shall incur one to three years' imprisonment."

The Article is so broad that it permits the imprisonment of adults who engage in consensual homosexual conduct in private. It also makes anyone involved in the non-violent advocacy of gay and lesbian rights vulnerable to charges of "promoting" homosexual acts.

Campaigners demonstrate in favor of equalising
the age of consent in the UK. London, 1996

In the Nicaraguan Supreme Court ruling that upheld the law as constitutional, sodomy is defined in a confused manner as "a sexual inversion, that is anal copulation between two persons of the male sex or between two women...a deviation from normal life which subverts the foundations of a correct society, attached to ethical principles for the well-being of the family and the nation as a whole...a threat to the holy institution of matrimony and procreation." The ruling goes on to say that "to authorise its free practice would be a legal attack on the growth of the Nicaraguan population and a setback to its political, economic and social advancement."[22]

Romania is the only European country that still criminalises homosexual acts. Like many other nations of Eastern and Central Europe, Romania recently joined the Council of Europe. Its entry, in

October 1993, was made conditional on a number of aspects of Romanian domestic law being brought into line with the *European Convention for the Protection of Human Rights,* including its legislation criminalising homosexual acts. Romania's penal code (article 200, paragraph 1), makes consensual adult homosexual activity a crime punishable by up to five years imprisonment. While this law has not been used to prosecute lesbians since the 1960s, Romania alone among non-Islamic countries specifically criminalizes homosexual acts between women as well as men.

In 1996 the Romanian parliament ignored widespread appeals from a number of countries, and from human rights organisations including Amnesty International, calling for the repeal of Article 200. Instead the scope of the legislation was extended. New articles were added allowing for the arrest, prosecution and imprisonment of people involved in same-sex acts in private between consenting adults if they cause "a public scandal". Such acts are punishable by prison sentences of one to five years. Another broadly-worded paragraph was added making "public enticement or incitement to homosexual behaviour" a crime punishable by the same sentence.

In Zimbabwe homosexuality is criminalised under the common law concerning unnatural offences and sodomy. In 1995, Gays and

Euan Sutherland (above) and Chris Morris, took the UK to the European court of Human Rights in December 1996

Lesbians of Zimbabwe (GALZ), a multiracial group campaigning for lesbian and gay rights, applied for a stall at the International Book Fair in Harare. Their application was denied. At the time, President Robert Mugabe is quoted in *The Guardian* as saying:

> *"I find it extremely outrageous and repugnant to my human conscience that such repulsive organisations, like those of homosexuals who offend both against the laws of nature and the morals and religious beliefs espoused by our society, should have any advocate in our midst and even elsewhere in the world...if we accept homosexuality as a right, as is being argued by the association of sodomites and sexual perverts, what moral fibre shall our society ever have to deny organised drug addicts, or even those given to bestiality, the rights they might claim and allege they possess under the rubric of individual freedom' and human rights' including the freedom to write, publish and publicise their literature on them."*

In 1996, GALZ challenged the ban in high court where Judge Wilson Sandura overturned it, granting the group the right to set up its stand at the fair. When news of this decision reached the public, a group calling itself Sangano Munhumutapa from the University of Zimbabwe threatened to burn down all the stands in the fair if GALZ participated. A number of churches also protested and a leading official of the ruling political party, the Zimbabwean African National Union-Patriotic Front, reportedly also made threats.

On 31 July 1996, the day before the fair opened, the Zimbabwe authorities (the Board of Censors and the Ministry of Home Affairs) issued an official order under Section 17 (1) of the *Censorship and Entertainments Control* Act banning GALZ from participating in the fair, in order to "protect the cultural health" of Zimbabwe. The GALZ publications which were to be displayed dealt with a range of human rights issues relating to homosexuality, a pamphlet from the Catholic church, and advice about counselling services. These were defined as "undesirable", or likely to be associated with breaches of the peace, or disorderly or immoral behaviour. Anyone defying the order, including members of other organisations at the fair displaying GALZ literature, would be liable to two years imprisonment, fined Z$1000, or both. A mob of some hundred young demonstrators staged unruly and menacing demonstrations against gays and lesbians outside the fair, threatening to kill GALZ activists on a number of occasions. At the end of the fair, the GALZ stand was ransacked by the mob, literature was torn up, and the stall burned while the police stood by refusing to intervene. Police protection had been requested, but law enforcement officers said that gays and lesbians had no right to help if attacked.

Amnesty International condemned the denial of freedom of expression to GALZ and protested at Zimbabwe government inaction in trying to prevent the attacks, which amounted to condoning such abuse.[23]

Twenty-eight of the fifty United States have repealed their criminal "sodomy" statutes since 1962. In other states such statutes are being challenged by human rights organisations. Texas, Kansas, Missouri, Montana, and Tennessee apply their sodomy laws only to homosexuals. Although these discriminatory laws have not been used recently for detention, Amnesty International would consider anyone imprisoned under them a prisoner of conscience, and is actively campaigning for their repeal.[24]

Gay victim of hate crime killing, Texas

39

"The laws forbidding homosexual acts often act as a kind of mandate for violations... They have killed gays and lesbians in Texas because they believe (them) to be less than human. I believe it's very important that people understand why the murders happen and that such murder is as a result of hatred. It is committed by young teenage men. Those men were not born haters. They were taught to hate by a society that continues to pass laws against lesbians and gay men, that continues to demonise lesbians and gays, that preaches hatred from the pulpit."

Anne, human rights campaigner, Texas

Where homosexuality is a criminal offence it can also be used as a pretext to imprison or punish other prisoners of conscience. The writer and satirist Ali-Akbar Saidi Sirjani was arrested in Iran in March 1994. He had written to the Iranian authorities objecting to the censorship of dissenting voices in Iran. Most of his writings had been effectively banned. His arrest followed accusations in the official press of his involvement with "espionage networks in the West, drug abuse, brewing alcohol, receiving money from counter-revolutionary circles and homosexuality". He was held in

© Maxine Young, International PEN

Iranian writer Ali-Akbar Saidi Sirjani, charged with espionage, drug abuse, brewing alcohol, and homosexuality, was sentenced to death.

40

incommunicado detention. In November 1994 he was reported to have died of a heart attack.[25]

**Prisoners of Conscience Detained for the
Advocacy of Homosexual Rights**
Amnesty International's campaigning for the release of prisoners of conscience includes work for the release of anyone imprisoned solely for their actual or alleged homosexuality, as well as anyone facing detention for their peaceful advocacy of the rights of homosexuals. They may be detained under laws specifically aimed at the criminalisation of homosexuality or under laws regarding public behaviour and morality which may be used to target lesbians and gay men.

In Turkey, following the suicide of a transvestite in Istanbul, several transvestites held a press conference on 7 December 1989 at the Yeni Bizans (New Byzantine) Cultural Centre, owned by Ibrahim Eren. That evening Ibrahim Eren was arrested for violation of Law 2911 (Article 536 of the penal code) and charged with "the illegal distribution of leaflets in public places". He was sent to Bayrampasa Prison in Istanbul. Two other transvestite activists, Ahmet Oğuz Akdoğan and Aydin Mentese, were indicted along with Ibrahim Eren, but not imprisoned.

In Greece, Irene Petropoulou, editor of the gay and lesbian

© Amnesty International

Gerardo Rubén Ortega Zurita and José Cruz Reyes Potenciano

41

magazine Amphi, was sentenced to five months' imprisonment and a 50,000 drachma fine on charges of violating Articles 29, 30 and 31 of Law 5060/1931 of the Greek penal code because of an article that she published in an issue of the magazine in 1991. The article, a comment in the classified section, asked why so many homosexual and heterosexual men were interested in corresponding with lesbians. The court ruled that the comment offended "public feelings of decency and sexual morals and cannot be considered a work of art and science". Amnesty International expressed concern about Irene Petropoulou's sentence, and would have considered her a prisoner of conscience had she been imprisoned. She was acquitted by the Athens Appeal Court in 1993.[26]

In Mexico, Gerardo Rubén Ortega Zurita and José Cruz Reyes Potenciano, two gay activists well known in Mexico City for their voluntary AIDS prevention work amongst the city's male prostitutes, were arrested in June 1992 by members of the Federal Judicial Police, accused of the rape and sexual assault of a minor. Their arrest was announced to the press before they had been formally charged. Both were reportedly beaten by the police and held incommunicado until the next day. Medical examinations carried out on the day of arrest on both men reportedly certified that their injuries were consistent with the allegations of beatings by the police. On their transfer to a prison in Mexico City, pending their trial, both reportedly suffered beatings and harassment from other prison inmates. On 31 March 1993, they were sentenced to thirteen years and nine months' imprisonment. Amnesty International appealed to the Mexican authorities, concerned that these men appeared to have been prisoners of conscience held solely for their advocacy of the rights of members of Mexico's gay community, their active campaigning on gay issues, and their outspoken criticism of alleged police abuse of homosexuals, and called for an inquiry into their reported abuse in detention. On 9 July 1993, Zurita and Potenciano were released following a successful appeal, and cleared of all charges.[27]

Prisoners of Conscience Detained for Their Homosexual Identity or Homosexual Acts

Arrests and detentions of gays simply because they are gay continue to be reported from many parts of the world. In Romania, between 1993 and 1995 at least eleven people were imprisoned under legislation criminalising consensual homosexual acts between consenting adults in private.

Two young gay men from Timisoara, Mirel Ciprian Cucu and Milorad (Marian) Mutascu, who had been living together in a flat, were arrested in January 1993. They were placed in preventative detention. Mirel Cucu was charged under Article 200, paragraph 1, of the Romanian Penal Code. He faced a possible prison sentence of one to five years for "having sexual relations with a person of the same sex". Milorad Mutascu was charged under paragraph 2 of the same article, for having homosexual relations with a minor. He faced a possible prison sentence of two to seven years, (a heterosexual relationship between people of the same ages as Cucu and Mutascu would have been lawful). In April Amnesty International called for their immediate release. They were adopted as prisoners of conscience. Both were released after two months' imprisonment, pending their trial. In June 1993 they were tried by the county court of Timisoara, and received suspended sentences of one and two years imprisonment, respectively. The two men had also faced vilification in the official police newspaper, *Tim-polis*, which published their names, photos, and addresses even before formal charges had been brought against them. The paper described their

© Amnesty International

Prisoner of Conscience Milorad Mutascu 1992

43

relationship as a "social danger". According to a recent account in the UK magazine *Gay Times*, Milorad Mutascu was unable to find work because of his "criminal" history. He committed suicide in August 1995. The monument on his grave has been defaced. Cyprian Cucu sought political asylum in the United States. The story of the two men has been dramatised in the film *November Dream*.

In 1993 the Romanian authorities sentenced three men, Marius Aitai, Cosmin Hutanu, and Ovidiu Chetea, to up to two-and-a-half years' imprisonment for having sex in private. Amnesty International

© Amnesty International

Peter Duffy QC of Amnesty International argued against
Botswana's laws criminalising homosexuality. 1996

considered them to be prisoners of conscience and called for their immediate and unconditional release. They were among fifty-seven people detained in Romanian prisons who had been convicted under Article 200 paragraph 1 of the Romanian criminal code at that time.[28]

Even where prosecutions are rarely reported, the criminalisation of same-sex relationships can provide a permanent source of anxiety to gay men and lesbians by holding over them a constant threat of prosecution. It can also figure in civil proceedings even when no criminal charges have been brought.

In Botswana, Sections 164a and 16, of the Botswana penal code prohibit "carnal knowledge against the laws of nature". Homosexual acts are punishable by up to two years in jail. Utjiwa Kanane, a Botswanan citizen, and Graham Norrie, a British national, were arrested in Maun, northeast Botswana, on 26 December 1994. Charges of "carnal knowledge against the order of nature" were brought against them. The British man was fined and expelled from the country in March 1995. Utjiwa Kanane lodged an appeal against the charges against him on the basis that Articles 164a and 167 of the Botswana Penal Code violate: 1) the right to privacy, to freedom of association, and to non-discrimination on the basis of sex that are guaranteed in the Botswanan Constitution, and 2) Botswana's obligations as a state party to the International Covenant on Civil and Political Rights.

At the time of writing, Kanane's case is to be heard in the High Court of Botswana in Francistown in December 1996. The constitutional case will be argued by Peter Duffy QC, a former Chair of the International Executive Committee of Amnesty International.[29]

In the United States in 1993, a Virginia court denied Sharon Bottoms, a lesbian, custody of her two-year-old son. It is reported that the court referred to the state's criminal sodomy statute in declaring her an "unfit parent." These state laws have been upheld by the US Supreme Court. In the 1986 case of *Bowers v. Hardwick*, the court upheld the constitutionality of Georgia's criminal sodomy statute, stating that the US Constitution does not guarantee a "fundamental right to homosexuals to engage in acts of consensual sodomy." However, in 1992 the Kentucky Supreme Court in *Commonwealth v. Wasson* found that the state's criminal sodomy law violated the "right to privacy" embodied in the Kentucky State constitution, and denied equal protection of the law to homosexuals.[30]

Other Criminal Legislation Used to Imprison Lesbians and Gay Men

Although in some countries homosexuality is not specifically criminalised, the absence of these laws does not necessarily safeguard the basic human rights of lesbians and gay men. People continue to be harassed and arbitrarily detained solely by reason of their sexual orientation. In many places, people suspected of homosexual behaviour are detained on ambiguous criminal charges ranging from vagrancy to "hooliganism," or detained without charge or trial under systems of administrative detention.

In China, prior to November 1992, homosexuals were harassed by the police and sent to "re-education through labour" camps, a form of administrative detention not requiring a judicial process. Some were also reportedly sentenced to terms of imprisonment under the criminal law on charges such as "disturbing social order" and "hooliganism." A Canton newspaper reported in February 1992 that a man was sentenced to eight years in jail for having homosexual relations with other men. In another case, two women who had been living together as partners in Anhui province were detained for fifteen days on charges of "unruly behaviour" while the case was referred to a higher authority. In April 1992, the Ministry of Public Security decided to release the women, finding that there was no legal basis on which to prosecute them.

In November 1992 it was reported that the Chinese Communist Party no longer regarded homosexuality as an offence, and that provincial police departments were instructed not to arrest homosexuals. Current policies on the treatment of lesbians and gay men are unclear and vary from region to region. Since the 1992 change in law, Amnesty International has received reports of cases in which people have been imprisoned in connection with their homosexuality.[31]

The Death Penalty
International human rights standards recognise each person's right not to be arbitrarily deprived of their life, nor to be subjected to torture or to cruel, inhuman, or degrading treatment or punishment. International standards also call for the gradual abolition of the death penalty. Amnesty International opposes the death penalty in all circumstances. The organisation seeks to bring attention to cases where capital punishment is used in a discriminatory manner, such as against persons based on their sexual, racial, or ethnic identity.

Although referred to as a "punishment" for crime, the death penalty is often used arbitrarily as a tool for political repression or disproportionately imposed on the poor and powerless. Like members of other disenfranchised groups, lesbians and gay men are sometimes sentenced to death on the grounds of their identity.

In Iran, under Islamic law, sodomy is classed among the crimes considered *hodoud* (against the divine will, liable to divine retribution) and is subject to a mandatory death sentence. Involvement in a lesbian relationship can cost a woman her life: If a woman is convicted four times for *mosahegeh* – lesbianism – she faces the death penalty. A lesser punishment for the offence is one hundred and eight lashes for each person. Lesbianism must be proved by the testimony – *qassameh* – "of four righteous men who might have observed it."

During 1995 at least fifty people were executed in Iran. It is unclear how many of these executions may have resulted from accusations of homosexuality. However, in November 1995 Mehdi Barazandeh, a Dervish mystic, was reported to have been stoned to death for adultery and sodomy in Hamadan.

> *"For homosexual men or women Islam has proscribed the most severe punishments...After it has been proved on the basis of Sharia, they should seize him (or her), they should keep him standing, they should split him in two with a sword, they should either cut off his head or they should split him from the head... He will fall down... After he is dead, they should bring logs, make a fire and place the corpse on the top, set fire to it and burn it, or it should be taken to a mountain and thrown down. Then the parts of the corpse should be gathered together and burned. Or they should dig a hole, make a fire in the hole, and throw him alive into the fire. We do not have such punishments for other offences."*
>
> Ayatollah Musava-Ardebili, Teheran University, Iran 32

Amnesty International has received reports that some lesbians and gay men in Iran have faced punishments such as execution or lashes for their homosexuality, but they have been extremely difficult to substantiate.

In July 1980, a thirty-eight-year-old man, married with six children, was stoned to death in the town of Kerman in southern Iran. He had been convicted of homosexuality and adultery. In a number of recent cases, homosexuality has been used as one of the pretexts for

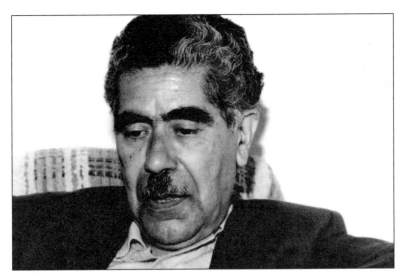

Dr Ali Mozaffarian, Iranian surgeon, executed for homosexuality
and adultery, Shiraz, 1992

application of the death penalty. Dr. Ali Mozaffarian, a well-known
surgeon and one of the leaders of the Sunni Muslim community in
Fars province in southern Iran, was executed in Shiraz in early August
1992. He was convicted of spying for the United States and Iraq, as
well as "adultery and sodomy". His videotaped "confessions", which
may have been obtained as a result of physical or psychological
pressure, were broadcast on television. Amnesty International believes
that his trial may have been unfair, and that the charges of spying,
adultery and homosexuality were merely used to target this Sunni
Muslim leader.[33]

In other Islamic countries where *hodoud* offenses are prosecuted,
homosexuality may also be punishable by death. Under the revised
penal code in Mauritania (1983), the death penalty is prescribed for
male Muslims convicted of certain acts of the *hadd* offence of
homosexuality. In the Arab Republic of Yemen sodomy is specified
as a *hadd* offence punishable by execution. Lesbians and gay men
may be vulnerable to human rights abuses in other states where
Sharia is the basis for penal codes including Saudi Arabia, Pakistan,
Oman and Sudan.

In January 1997, British journalist Jonathan Steele interviewed the governor of Kandahar, Afghanistan, Mohammed Hassan, one of the leading mullahs of the Taliban. Hassan explained the leaders of the school of Islamic thought in Kandahar were divided about the appropriate punishment for male homosexuality. One group of scholars believed that homosexuals should be taken to the top of the highest building in the city and thrown off; another group thought they should be buried alive; while a third argued that they should merely be put on public display for a few hours with blackened faces. This was his own favourite solution. "We have punished people this way in Kandahar," he told Steele. "Homosexuality is a very big crime."

Unfair Capital Trials

Each year unfair trials violate the fundamental rights of political prisoners throughout the world. The requirements which guarantee the right to a fair, prompt, and public hearing before an independent and impartial tribunal for legal proceedings are set out in the *International Covenant on Civil and Political Rights* and other international human rights treaties. In its work in support of fair trials for political prisoners, Amnesty International sometimes finds that a person's real or alleged sexual orientation can work to his or her disadvantage in an unfair trial. Sometimes charges founded on allegations of homosexual behaviour will also be used by governments as a pretext to discredit critics, as in Iran for example.

Amnesty International is concerned about unfair capital trials when allegations of homosexuality are accepted by judge or jury as factors relevant to the culpability of the accused.

In the United States, Janice Buttrum was convicted of murder and sentenced to death. She was seventeen years old at the time of the crime. By the time of the trial, much publicity had been generated in the local press about her case. Her sexuality was presented to the jury in an inflammatory manner. The defence asked for a change of trial venue, which was not granted. During the sentencing hearing, a private psychologist appeared as a witness for the state. Although he had not interviewed Janice Buttrum, he testified that she was a bisexual sadist, who would commit other violent sexual acts in the

Homophobia influenced the trial of Calvin Burdine,
a gay man now on death row in Texas

future. (She had only one previous conviction for a minor offence, not involving sexual violence.) She was sentenced to death in 1981. On appeal, this was commuted to life imprisonment on the grounds that she had not received a fair hearing.[34]

Also in the United States, Calvin Burdine, a gay man, was convicted of murder in Texas in 1983. He was on trial for his life in circumstances in which his sexual orientation appears to have influenced the jury. His court-appointed defence lawyer, Joe Frank Cannon, fell asleep during the proceedings on numerous occasions In addition, he made remarks during the hearing that were openly hostile to homosexuals. During a court hearing in 1988 he referred to homosexuals as "queers" and "fairies". He failed to object to three members of the jury who had admitted that they were prejudiced against homosexuals. He also failed to object when the prosecutor asserted that to "send a homosexual to the penitentiary certainly isn't a very bad punishment for a homosexual". At the time of writing Calvin Burdine remains on death row.[35]

Abuses Based on Real or Perceived HIV Status
Gay men are mistakenly blamed for the occurrence of Human Immuno-Deficiency Virus/Acquired Immuno-Deficiency Syndrome (HIV/AIDS) resulting in increased discrimination and abuse aimed at

homosexuals. Gay men are often considered to be "AIDS carriers", and as a result may be subjected to ill-treatment at the hands of government authorities. In addition, activists who are working to prevent the spread of the AIDS virus in gay communities may be targeted for human rights abuses.

In El Salvador, Amnesty International was concerned for the safety of Wilfredo Valencia Palacios, President of *Entre Amigos*, a gay men's group, and deputy director of the Oscar Romero AIDS Project in San Salvador. His work involved preventive health education among male and female prostitutes and transvestites in the shanty towns and marginalised communities of the national capital. On 29 October 1994 he was stopped and beaten up by two unidentified men in plain clothes who told him his work was "against God's designs" and that if AIDS did not kill the "faggots" they themselves would do it. If he came back to the area to look for them, they said, he would be "a dead man". A week later two men, believed to belong to an anti-gay "death squad", approached him and asked if he was distributing condoms. He said this was part of his AIDS prevention work. Gunshots were then fired and he was followed in a car, being warned that he had thirty days to leave the country. In July 1995 *Entre Amigos* received three death threats from an anti-homosexual death squad *La Sombra Negra* (Black Shadow), threatening to come to the next meeting of the gay group to kill them all. The files of the AIDS Project, FUNDASIDA, were raided. Confidential files including the names of Entre Amigos members were stolen. Members of the group went into hiding.

The UN-appointed commission *Grupo Conjunto*, which investigated illegal armed groups in El Salvador in 1994, considered that these squads were composed of former or current members of the police or army who carry out acts of "private justice", settling old political scores and undertaking "social cleansing operations" against marginalised sectors of society.[36]

In Nicaragua, activists campaigning for AIDS awareness and providing safer sex information to lesbians and gay men were concerned that their visibility and prominence had prompted an anti-gay backlash in the country. They believed that they may have been considered to be "promoting" homosexuality, and thus be eligible for imprisonment under Nicaragua's anti-sodomy law of 1992 which states that: "anyone who induces, promotes, propagandises or practices in scandalous form sexual intercourse between persons of the same sex commits the crime of sodomy and shall incur 1 to 3 years' imprisonment".[37]

The first Congress of Homosexual Solidarity was to be held in Istanbul from 2-6 July 1993. The Congress was banned at the last minute by the Governor of Istanbul who said that it would be contrary to the "traditions and moral values" of Turkish society and might disturb the peace. On 3 July 1993, Turkish and international delegates planning to attend the Congress decided to hold a press conference in protest at the ban. Three Turkish activists, Huseyin Kuş kaya, Cem Özipek and Onur Sarvaut, were arrested before the press conference.

Twenty-eight foreign delegates were detained by the police on their way to the press conference, or at their hotel. They were initially taken to a local police station, threatened with strip searching, and held in a police bus for most of the day. As they were on their way to the airport to be deported their bus was diverted to a local hospital where they were told they would have to submit to a blood test for HIV. They refused to permit blood to be drawn. Ultimately the authorities withdrew their demand and they were finally deported to Germany. The sole motivation of the attempts to submit them to strip searches and blood tests appears to have been to punish or humiliate them for their homosexuality and gay rights advocacy.[38]

These are just a few examples of how the incorrect linkage of HIV status and homosexual activity become the basis of abuse.

Notes to Part 1

1. AI Index: AMR 41/0 7/94
2. AI Index: AMR 23/46/93, Homophobia Homicide' AIUK leaflet on Colombia, 1994.
3. AI Index: AMR 19/07/93
4. AI Index: AMR 19/07/93
5. Amnesty International Annual Report, 1995
6. AI Index: AMR 46/19/94
7. AI Index: EUR 39/01/95
8. AI Index: EUR 39/02/94, EUR 39/01/85
9. AI Index: AMR 46/15/96
10. AI Index : NWS 11/13/92
11. AI Index: AMR 51/36/96
12. AI Index: MDE 23/11/9
13. AI Index: EUR 44/65/93
14. AI Index: EUR 44/65/93
15. AI Index: EUR/11/05/94
16. Amnesty International Report, 1993
17. AI Index: POL 30/01/94
18. AI Index: POL 30/01/94
19. AI Index: EUR 01/03/92
20. AI Index: POL 30/02/93
21. AI Index: POL 30/02/93
22. AI Index: NWS 11/27/92, NWS 11/32/92
23. AI Index: NWS 13 8/96
24. AI Index: AMR 51/25/95
25. AI Index: MDE 13/03/94
26. AI Index:ACT 77/12/95
27. AI Index: AMR 41/3/93
28. AI Index: EUR 39/01/95
29. AI Index: AFR 16/01/95, AIUK GLBT News 1 1996
30. AI Index: AMR 51/25/95
31. AI Index: POL 33/04/93
32. Human Rights are Women's Right, Amnesty International, 1995
33. AI Index: MDE 13/WUI/08/92, NWS 11/48/92 ADD
34. AI Index : AMR 51/23/91
35. AI Index: AMR 51/31/95, AMR 51/59/95
36. AI Index: AMR 29/13/94
37. AI Index: NWS 11/32/92
38. AI Index: EUR 44/65/93

Index numbers refer to AI documents available from the address inside the Front cover.

PART 2

LESBIAN AND GAY ORGANISATIONS WORKING FOR HUMAN RIGHTS

Organisations working for gay and lesbian rights have developed and evolved over time and in response to social pressure and discrimination. Organisations which promote the rights of lesbians and gay men have formed on all continents. Some of the countries where gay and lesbian groups currently exist include: Albania, Argentina, Brazil, Canada, Chile, Colombia, Finland, France, Ghana, Hungary, India, Indonesia, Ireland, Malaysia, Mexico, Norway, Peru, the Philippines, South Africa, Thailand, the United Kingdom, the United States, and Zimbabwe. These organisations have various goals and purposes. But all are fighting for the observance of the basic human rights of an overlooked minority. Amnesty International includes information here about the work of these organisations to show the range of work presently being done to protect the human rights of lesbians and gay men. This section is by no means comprehensive or representative; there are many more organisations than those discussed below.

In North America, gay and lesbian organisations are plentiful. In Canada, gay and lesbian organisations have fought successfully to have sexual orientation included in the Federal Human Rights Act. In 1994 Amnesty International USA's "Breaking the Silence" Campaign brought Amnesty International volunteers together to work against the "sodomy" laws of five states in the USA which only apply to men. Lesbians and gay men in the United States have been fighting against the "sodomy" laws and also against a host of state and municipal challenges to equal rights protections. In addition, gay and lesbian groups such as the Community United Against Violence in San Francisco are working to end anti-gay hate crimes. In addition to the domestic-focused gay rights groups that seek to

© Donna Binder, Impact Visuals

Lesbian victims of homophobic attacks in the
"USA breaking the Silence Campaign" 1994

protect the lives of lesbians and gay men, a number of other organisations have added international concerns to their work, such as the Lambda Legal Defence's immigration and asylum project.

Gay and lesbian Latino/as have organised La Red, a network that works in solidarity with organisations in Latin America. Gay Native Americans have organised to combat the double-discrimination they face as Native Americans and as homosexuals.

Whilst a number of governments of the South portray gay and lesbian rights as a concept alien to their culture and people, gay and lesbian groups have proliferated in Latin America, Africa and Asia.

There are many strong gay and lesbian organisations in Latin America. In Mexico, *Circulo Cultural Gay* has organised protests against the recent wave of assassinations aimed at gay men and transvestites including the Chiapas assasinations of gay men in the early 1990's. Their work has been supported by many other gay and lesbian organisations, as well as the Department of Human Rights of the Archdiocese of Mexico. In Peru, the Movimiento Homosexual de Lima is working against human rights abuse of the gay community both from the police and agents of the state and from the armed opposition. In Brazil, the Grupo Gay da Bahia has reported that 1200 lesbians and gay men may have been killed since 1980, many by death squads.

Colombia's Proyecto Dignidade was formed in 1994 to expose violations against desechables "disposable people" including homosexuals.

In Chile the Corporacion Chilena de Prevencion del SIDA challenged the dismissal of workers on grounds of their HIV status. In Costa Rica in May 1995 Triangula Rosa was recognised as the first legally recognised organisation for lesbians, gay men and transgendered people. In Cuba Grupo de Action por la Libertad de Expresion de la Eleccion Sexual is a Cuban NGO which works against discrimination against people on grounds of their sexuality.

Homosexuals for Liberation is an Argentinian gay rights group that has been campaigning alongside the Mothers of the Plaza de Mayo to find out the truth about what happened to some 30,000 people who were "disappeared" under military rule during the "Dirty War" between 1976 and 1983, and to bring those responsible to justice.

© David Harrad, Gay Times

Gay Pride, Rio de Janeiro, 1993

Lesbianas a la Vista is an Argentinian group demonstrating for lesbian rights as human rights. In 1995 Media Luna was launched as the first lesbian group to be organised in El Salvador.

In the Caribbean, gay and lesbian organisations are working in several countries. In the Dominican Republic, gay men and lesbians report that they are vulnerable to harassment under laws that proscribe "offences against morality," but several groups for lesbians and gay men have formed. One such group is the lesbian group, the Colectivo Ciguay, which works against discrimination and harassment. The Gay Freedom Movement of Jamaica has been publishing a magazine since the 1970s.

In Africa, there are gay and lesbian organisations in many countries. An earlier chapter of this book records some of the struggles of Gays and Lesbians of Zimbabwe (GALZ) against social and political discrimination, laws that outlaw homosexuality and widespread homophobic attitudes. In Nigeria, the Gentlemen's Alliance, a group of gay men, held the country's first gay conference in 1991, despite the presence of a law that makes "carnal knowledge against the order of nature" punishable by up to fourteen years' imprisonment. In Ghana, the Afro Lesbian and Gay Club works against laws that ban "unnatural carnal knowledge" punishable by up to three years in jail. In South Africa, the Gay and Lesbian Organisation of Witwatersrand and other gay and lesbian groups worked to ensure inclusion of civil rights protection for gay man and lesbians in the country's new constitution in 1996.

Lesbians and gay men are organising throughout Asia and the Pacific. In South Asia, lesbians and gay men have banded together to campaign against Section 377 of India's Penal Code, which bans "carnal intercourse against the order of nature," and which organisers say leads to harassment of gay men in India. The regional coalition working against Section 377 includes Bombay Dost, Sakhi, and Arambh of India; Action for AIDS of Singapore; FACT of Thailand; KKLGN of Indonesia; The Library Fund from the Philippines; and the Malaysian group Pink Triangle. In Sri Lanka Companions on a Journey, a gay rights group, organised a conference in 1996 entitled: "Emerging Gay Identities in Sri Lanka". In December 1995 GAY NUSANTARA organised the Second

Japanese Gay Pride demonstration, Tokyo 1995

Indonesian Lesbian and Gay Congress. In the Philippines the Progressive Organisation of Gays in the Philippines organised the country's first Gay Pride March in June 1995. The Asian Lesbian Network, which met for the first time in 1990, includes lesbian groups from Bangladesh, India, Indonesia, Japan, Malaysia, Singapore and Thailand, as well as Asian lesbian groups from the US, the UK, the Netherlands and Australia. These groups are working to define and combat the discrimination they face in their varied cultures.

In Western Europe, there are many well-organised and highly developed gay and lesbian organisations. Because gay and lesbian conduct is legal in nearly all Western European states, many of these movements are targeting various other forms of discrimination.

In the United Kingdom, the Stonewall Group compiled a dossier on anti-homosexual discrimination in the European Community where the list of complaints included discrimination in employment, the existence of anti-gay harassment, and problems of freedom of movement within the European Community. The organisation led the campaign against Clause 28 in the United Kingdom which bans the promotion of homosexuality as a "pretend family relationship" in schools. Stonewall campaigned for the same age of consent for heterosexual and homosexual sex in the UK in 1994, and has worked against discrimination against homosexuals in the armed forces.

Irish lesbian and gay groups scored a victory in their campaign to repeal the law criminalising consensual sex between men in private when the Irish Government published the Criminal Law Bill of 1993.

In Sweden, the lesbian and gay organisation, RFSL, has assisted gay and lesbian refugees in their quest for political asylum in that country. The RFSL has been successful in a number of these cases, assisting homosexuals from the Middle East, Asia, and Latin America to receive asylum based on their membership of a persecuted group.

In Greece, the lesbian and gay group, AKOE, provides support for lesbians and gay men within the country, protests anti-gay acts, and networks with other Mediterranean gay men and lesbians. In the Netherlands, black lesbians formed Fiida, a group which works to combat discrimination based on sexual orientation and race.

Lesbians and gay men in Turkey organised the Radical Gay Group, which works against discrimination and human rights abuses carried out by the authorities against the gay community.

In Eastern Europe, lesbian and gay organisations are growing in the wake of the political changes since the fall of the Berlin Wall. In Poland, for example, the first gay and lesbian organisation, Lambda, was officially registered in February 1990. Prior to this, in 1988, Homers Lambda, a Hungarian group, became the first officially recognised gay and lesbian organisation in Eastern Europe. The group reported on a wave of anti-gay violence, and protested the maintenance of "pink lists" by the Hungarian police, reportedly used to track homosexuals. In Latvia, lesbians and gay men who organised the Latvian Association for Sexual Equality celebrated in

1992 when Article 124.1 of the penal code, which had banned consensual sex between adult men, was repealed. Shogata Gay Albania campaigned successfully for the repeal of legislation criminalising homosexuality. In Croatia, Lesbians and Gay Men in Action set up an emergency centre in Zagreb for fleeing Bosnian gay men and lesbians. This centre provided emergency shelter, counselling and humanitarian aid.

In the Middle East, there are very few gay and lesbian organisations. In Muslim countries, homosexuals rarely organise themselves according to gay or lesbian identities. An organisation of Farsi-speaking lesbians and gay men has formed in Europe, with chapters in Sweden, the United Kingdom and Germany. HOMAN works for the rights of Farsi-speaking and Iranian lesbians and gay men, and is concerned with reports of executions of lesbians and gay men in Iran. Some members of this group are gay refugees, who work to spread the word about other Iranians who have suffered at the hands of the authorities. In Israel, there are several gay and lesbian organisations. One of the most well-known, the Society for the Protection of Personal Rights, works for legislation to protect lesbians and gay men.

Non-governmental organisations (NGOs) play a crucial role in the promotion and protection of human rights. International non-governmental organisations carry out independent investigations, monitor and criticise the official reports presented by states and international bodies, and publicly expose gross violations of human rights.

In recent years, specifically gay and lesbian organisations such as the International Lesbian and Gay Association (ILGA), the International Gay and Lesbian Youth Association and the International Gay and Lesbian Human Rights Commission have emerged to document human rights violations against gays and lesbians and to build international bridges among homosexual groups. In 1993, the Economic and Social Committee of the United Nations (ECOSOC), agreed to grant consultative status to ILGA, giving the organisation, among other things, the opportunity to present information on human rights abuses against homosexuals officially to intergovernmental human rights bodies.

In a positive trend, mainstream human rights NGOs which have been traditionally concerned with monitoring human rights violations are beginning to join international efforts to secure the rights of lesbians and gay men.

It is hoped that the efforts by Amnesty International to publicise human rights violations based on sexual orientation will contribute to placing these violations squarely on to the agendas of human rights organisations, the United Nations and other inter-governmental bodies.

PART 3

A ROLE FOR AMNESTY INTERNATIONAL IN PROTECTING THE RIGHTS OF GAY MEN AND LESBIANS

As a grassroots, international human rights organisation, Amnesty International plays a vital and unique role in locating gay and lesbian rights within the human rights debate, not as special rights to freedom from discrimination on grounds of sexual orientation, but as fundamental rights of each and every member of society.

Amnesty International defends the right of all people to physical and psychological integrity and to their freedom to hold and express their conscientiously held beliefs. It campaigns against grave violations of these rights by governments. As sexual orientation is a fundamental dimension of human identity, the work of Amnesty International can contribute to the full protection of people, in their most basic and private selves, as well as in their public identities.

Raising awareness among the public about human rights and the protection and promotion of the inherent dignity of the person free from fear of governmental persecution is an essential part of Amnesty International's mission. While the mandate of Amnesty International focuses on some of the gravest abuses of civil and political rights, the organisation supports and seeks to strengthen the international standards protecting the full range of human rights: economic, social, and cultural, as well as civil and political. Human rights awareness and education on all these issues is an important part of the work of Amnesty International human rights activists in their own countries.

Amnesty International's Evolving Mandate
Since its early years, Amnesty International has worked against torture, ill-treatment and execution of prisoners, against

"disappearances", and for fair and prompt trials for political prisoners, work that it has carried out without regard to the sexual orientation of the victims. Since its inception in 1961, Amnesty International has modified both the focus of its mandate and the forms of its actions to specifically support the advancement of gay and lesbian human rights:

In 1979 Amnesty International specifically affirmed that those imprisoned for advocating lesbian and gay rights would be considered prisoners of conscience.

In 1982 the organisation condemned forcible "medical" treatment carried out on people in detention against their will for the purpose of altering their sexual orientation.

In 1991 at the International Council Meeting in Yokohama, Japan, Amnesty International agreed to expand the scope of its work on behalf of imprisoned lesbians and gay men. Within its mandate, Amnesty International works for the release of prisoners of conscience men and women detained solely for their beliefs, colour, sex, ethnic origin, language or religion who have not used or advocated violence. At Yokohama the organisation decided to include amongst those it defined as prisoners of conscience people imprisoned solely because of their homosexual identity, whether their homosexuality is real or alleged, including the practice of homosexual acts carried out in private between consenting adults.

The Scope of Amnesty International's Work on Behalf of Gay Men and Lesbians

Amnesty International presses governments to uphold human rights and to bring national legislation into line with international standards. Thus it campaigns to repeal legislation that could result in the detention of prisoners of conscience on the basis of their sexual identity.

Amnesty International opposes torture and executions by governments in all cases. It takes action against deliberate and arbitrary killings, torture and hostage-taking by armed opposition groups. Thus Amnesty International works against any torture or killing, whether legally sanctioned or extrajudicially carried out, of anyone because of their sexual orientation.

Amnesty International works against the cruel, inhuman or degrading treatment of persons in detention in any situation. Thus it opposes the forcible "medical" treatment of lesbians and gay men in an attempt to change their sexual orientation.

Amnesty International works to prevent gay and lesbian asylum-seekers being forcibly returned "refouled" to countries where they might face abuses such as detention, torture, execution and "disappearance". It presses for fair hearings in the countries in which they request asylum. Additionally, it opposes barriers erected in asylum determination procedures in law or in practice against anyone solely because of their sexual orientation.

Amnesty International works to ensure fair trials for political prisoners. Thus the use of a person's status as a lesbian or gay man in an attempt to bias the judge or jury against them would be considered cause for concern.

Amnesty International is also concerned about unfair trials in capital criminal cases where the accused faces the death penalty. Thus it opposes allegations of homosexuality being used in ways that are likely to prejudice the judiciary.

Supporting the Work of Others for Dignity and Basic Rights
Amnesty International takes action in support of other human rights groups including the many different domestic and international groups that document abuses against lesbians and gay men.

Amnesty International membership structures around the world have an important task in reaching out, making links, exchanging information and developing solidarity with gay and lesbian groups and movements in their own communities and further afield, and working in solidarity with organisations campaigning for homosexual equality and justice both nationally and internationally.

Amnesty International members have an important educative function increasing public awareness about human rights and equality, and about violations against lesbians and gay men around the world, spreading awareness through a range of public education programmes.

Amnesty International members in many countries lobby for legislative changes in favor of homosexual equality and pressure their governments to comply with international standards in the treatment of gays and lesbians. At an intergovernmental level, Amnesty International can also help develop and monitor adherence to international standards relevant to the protection of gay men and lesbians.

Within Amnesty International's membership, important organising, campaigning and educative work is being undertaken by networks of lesbian and gay activists who are Amnesty members, like the Gay, Lesbian, Bisexual and Transgender (GLBT) Network in Amnesty International UK and similar groups in a number of other countries including the USA, France and Norway. Such networks undertake a range of targeted actions, show films, write articles, prepare exhibitions, distribute leaflets, organise meetings, lobby and campaign.

PART 4

AMNESTY INTERNATIONAL'S RECOMMENDATIONS FOR THE PROTECTION OF LESBIANS AND GAY MEN

Amnesty International recommends that governments:

- Release all prisoners of conscience immediately and unconditionally, including all persons imprisoned for their homosexual identity, for homosexual acts in private between consenting adults, for advocating the rights of homosexuals (including in the context of HIV/AIDS education), or for their political beliefs under the pretext of charges of homosexuality.

- Review all legislation and practices including sodomy laws (and revise or repeal where necessary) which result in the detention of persons because of their homosexual identity or homosexual acts in private between consenting adults. This review should also include any laws which result in imprisonment of advocates of homosexual rights.

- Stop the rape, sexual abuse and other torture and ill-treatment by governments of all persons, including lesbians and gay men. Cruel, inhuman or degrading treatment of persons in detention must be prohibited, including forcible "medical" treatment of lesbians or gay men in detention to change their sexual orientation.

- Stop the "disappearance" and extrajudicial execution of lesbians and gay men by government agents. Governments must immediately work to halt these abuses by conducting prompt, thorough and impartial investigations of all reports of killings or "disappearances" targeted at lesbians and gay men and bring those found responsible to justice.

- Abolish death penalty laws for all crimes, including those punishing homosexual acts or identity.

- Review laws and practices to ensure that torture, political killing, death threats and other grave harassment of persons, based on their sexual identity, are promptly and impartially investigated, prosecuted and punished in the regular administration of justice. Particular attention should be paid to ensuring that human rights defenders, working to protect the rights of homosexuals, or whose work in the context of women's human rights or HIV/AIDS education brings them under attack as lesbians or gay men, are adequately protected.

- Ensure that information on the prohibition against torture, including rape and sexual abuse, is fully included in the training of all agents of government, including all law enforcement personnel, civil or military; medical personnel; public officials and others involved in custody, interrogation, arrest and detention or imprisonment of individuals, including in the context of refugees and asylum-seekers. Special attention should be given in all training programmes to include protection of the rights of gay men and lesbians to be free of torture.

- Review and revise (or repeal where necessary) all barriers, whether in law or administrative practice, to persons seeking political asylum on the basis of persecution based on sexual orientation. Such barriers to the internationally guaranteed right to seek asylum would include discriminatory or exclusionary laws targeted towards homosexual orientation or unjustifiably linked to real or perceived HIV/AIDS status.

- Promote human rights education which emphasises the need to protect the human rights of all people, including lesbians and gay men.

- Work to ensure that protections for the human rights of gay men and lesbians are effectively advanced at all relevant UN conferences and in the work of its thematic mechanisms. Governments should encourage the national, regional and international participation of grassroots groups working to protect the human rights of gay men and lesbians and should include information on the protection of those rights in their national reports.

- Demonstrate their commitment to protecting the human rights of all persons, including lesbians and gay men, by ratifying the international instruments for the protection of human rights with as few limiting reservations as possible. These international instruments include:

  The International Covenant on Civil and Political Rights,
  The International Covenant on Economic, Social and Cultural Rights,
  The Convention Against Torture and Other Cruel, Inhuman and Degrading Treatment or Punishment,
  The Convention on the Elimination of All Forms of Discrimination Against Women,
  The Convention on the Elimination of All Forms of Racial Discrimination,
  The Convention on the Rights of the Child.

- When submitting reports to the appropriate international and regional treaty-monitoring bodies, governments should include information on: the ability of lesbians and gay men to enjoy the relevant rights and freedoms; steps being taken at national and local levels to remove obstacles to the full enjoyment of rights and freedoms by lesbians and gay men; and provisions for their protection.

APPENDIX

THE UNIVERSAL DECLARATION OF HUMAN RIGHTS

Adopted and proclaimed by General Assembly Resolution 217 A(III) 10 December 1948

Preamble

Whereas recognition of the inherent dignity and of the equal and inalienable rights of all members of the human family is the foundation of freedom, justice and peace in the world,

Whereas disregard and contempt for human rights have resulted in barbarous acts which have outraged the conscience of mankind, and the advent of a world in which human beings shall enjoy freedom of speech and belief and freedom from fear and want has been proclaimed as the highest aspiration of the common people,

Whereas it is essential, if man is not to be compelled to have recourse, as a last resort, to rebellion against tyranny and oppression, that human rights should be protected by the rule of law,

Whereas it is essential to promote the development of friendly relations between nations,

Whereas the peoples of the United Nations have in the Charter reaffirmed their faith in fundamental human rights, in the dignity and worth of the human person and in the equal rights of men and women and have determined to promote social progress and better standards of life in larger freedom,

Whereas Member States have pledged themselves to achieve, in co-operation with the United Nations, the promotion of universal respect for and observance of human rights and fundamental freedoms,

Whereas a common understanding of these rights and freedoms is of the greatest importance for the full realization of this pledge,

Now, therefore, The General Assembly Proclaims this Universal Declaration of Human Rights as a common standard of achievement for all peoples and all nations, to the end that every individual and every organ of society, keeping this Declaration constantly in mind, shall strive by teaching and education to promote respect for these rights and freedoms and by progressive measures, national and international, to secure their universal and effective recognition and observance, both among the peoples of Member States themselves and among the peoples of territories under their jurisdiction.

Article 1
All human beings are born free and equal in dignity and rights. They are endowed with reason and conscience and should act towards one another in a spirit of brotherhood.

Article 2
Everyone is entitled to all the rights and freedoms set forth in this Declaration, without distinction of any kind, such as race, colour, sex, language, religion, political or other opinion, national or social origin, property, birth or other status. Furthermore, no distinction shall be made on the basis of the political, jurisdictional or international status of the country or territory to which a person belongs, whether it be independent, trust, non-self-governing or under any other limitation of sovereignty.

Article 3
Everyone has the right to life, liberty and the security of person.

Article 4
No one shall be held in slavery or servitude; slavery and the slave trade shall be prohibited in all their forms.

Article 5
No one shall be subjected to torture or to cruel, inhuman or degrading treatment or punishment.

Article 6
Everyone has the right to recognition everywhere as a person before the law.

Article 7
All are equal before the law and are entitled without any discrimination to equal protection of the law. All are entitled to equal protection against any discrimination in violation of this Declaration and against any incitement to such discrimination.

Article 8
Everyone has the right to an effective remedy by the competent national tribunals for acts violating the fundamental rights granted him by the constitution or by law.

Article 9
No one shall be subjected to arbitrary arrest, detention or exile.

Article 10
Everyone is entitled in full equality to a fair and public hearing by an independent and impartial tribunal, in the determination of his rights and obligations and of any criminal charge against him.

Article 11
1. Everyone charged with a penal offence has the right to be presumed innocent until proved guilty according to law in a public trial at which he has had all the guarantees necessary for his defence.

2. No one shall be held guilty of any penal offence on account of any act or omission which did not constitute a penal offence, under national or international law, at the time when it was committed. Nor shall a heavier penalty be imposed than the one that was applicable at the time the penal offence was committed.

Article 12
No one shall be subjected to arbitrary interference with his privacy, family, home or correspondence, nor to attacks upon his honour and reputation. Everyone has the right to the protection of the law against such interference or attacks.

Article 13
1. Everyone has the right to freedom of movement and residence within the borders of each State.

2. Everyone has the right to leave any country, including his own, and to return to his country.

Article 14
1. Everyone has the right to seek and to enjoy in other countries asylum from persecution.

2. This right may not be invoked in the case of prosecutions genuinely arising from non-political crimes or from acts contrary to the purposes and principles of the United Nations.

Article 15
1. Everyone has the right to a nationality.

2. No one shall be arbitrarily deprived of his nationality nor denied the right to change his nationality.

Article 16
1. Men and women of full age, without any limitation due to race, nationality or religion, have the right to marry and to found a family. They are entitled to equal rights as to marriage, during marriage and at its dissolution.

2. Marriage shall be entered into only with the free and full consent of the intending spouses.

3. The family is the natural and fundamental group unit of society and is entitled to protection by society and the State.

Article 17
1. Everyone has the right to own property alone as well as in association with others.

2. No one shall be arbitrarily deprived of his property.

Article 18
Everyone has the right to freedom of thought, conscience and religion; this right includes freedom to change his religion or belief, and freedom, either alone or in community with others and in public or private, to manifest his religion or belief in teaching, practice, worship and observance.

Article 19
Everyone has the right to freedom of opinion and expression; this right includes freedom to hold opinions without interference and to seek, receive and impart information and ideas through any media and regardless of frontiers.

Article 20
1. Everyone has the right to freedom of peaceful assembly and association.

2. No one may be compelled to belong to an association.

Article 21
1. Everyone has the right to take part in the government of his country, directly or through freely chosen representatives.

2. Everyone has the right of equal access to public service in his country.

3. The will of the people shall be the basis of the authority of government; this will shall be expressed in periodic and genuine elections which shall be by universal and equal suffrage and shall be held by secret vote or by equivalent free voting procedures.

Article 22
Everyone, as a member of society, has the right to social security

and is entitled to realization, through national effort and international co-operation and in accordance with the organization and resources of each State. of the economic. social and cultural rights indispensable for his dignity and the free development of his personality.

Article 23
1. Everyone has the right to work, to free choice of employment, to just and favourable conditions of work and to protection against unemployment.

2. Everyone, without any discrimination, has the right to equal pay for equal work.

3. Everyone who works has the right to just and favourable remuneration ensuring for himself and his family an existence worthy of human dignity and supplemented, if necessary, by other means of social protection.

4. Everyone has the right to form and to join trade unions for the protection of his interests.

Article 24
Everyone has the right to rest and leisure, including reasonable limitation of working hours and periodic holidays with pay.

Article 25
1. Everyone has the right to a standard of living; adequate for the health and well-being of himself and of his family, including food, clothing, housing and medical care and necessary social services, and the right to security in the event of unemployment, sickness, disability, widowhood, old age or other lack of livelihood in circumstances beyond his control.

2. Motherhood and childhood are entitled to special care and assistance. All children, whether born in or out of wedlock, shall enjoy the same social protection.

Article 26

1. Everyone has the right to education. Education shall be free, at least in the elementary and fundamental stages. Elementary education shall be compulsory. Technical and professional education shall be made generally available and higher education shall be equally accessible to all on the basis of merit.

2. Education shall be directed to the full development of the human personality and to thestrengthening of respect for human rights and fundamental freedoms. It shall promote understanding, tolerance and friendship among all nations, racial or religious groups, and shall further the activities of the United Nations for the maintenance of peace.

3. Parents have a prior right to choose the kind of education that shall be given to their children.

Article 27

1. Everyone has the right freely to participate in the cultural life of the community, to enjoy the arts and to share in scientific advancement and its benefits.

2. Everyone has the right to the protection of the moral and material interests resulting from any scientific, literary or artistic production of which he is the author.

Article 28

Everyone is entitled to a social and international order in which the rights and freedoms set forth in this Declaration can be fully realised.

Article 29

1. Everyone has duties to the community in which alone the free and full development of his personality is possible.

2. In the exercise of his rights and freedoms, everyone shall be subject only to such limitations as are determined by law solely for the purpose of securing due recognition and respect for the rights and freedoms of others and of meeting the just requirements of morality, public order and the general welfare in a democratic society.

3. These rights and freedoms may in no case be exercised contrary to the purposes and principles of the United Nations.

Article 30
Nothing in this Declaration may be interpreted as implying for any State, group or person any right to engage in any activity or to perform any act aimed at the destruction of any of the rights and freedoms set forth herein.

APPENDIX

ROUGH GUIDE TO NATIONAL LEGISLATION ROUND THE WORLD ON THE LEGALITY OF HOMOSEXUAL ACTS

(This is not a definitive survey, but a rough guide to the state of legislation in relation to the criminalisation of homosexual acts in different countries. The survey is based largely on non-Amnesty International sources, and is, by its very nature, imprecise, partly because of the difficulty of access to information on law and practice on this issue in some countries, and partly because of the impossibility of comparing and matching very different legislative terms, definitions and arrangements.)

Sources
I   Index on Censorship: Laura Bruin 1995
p   The Third Pink Book (1993)
gl International Lesbian and Gay Association
h   Charles Humana. Human Rights Guide 1989
a   Recent Amnesty International information

COUNTRY	LAW includes date of decriminalisation, or Penal Code Article, and maximum sentence available if known	SOURCE
Afghanistan	Illegal for men and women. Sharia Law applies	I
Albania	Legal since 1994	a
Algeria	Illegal for men and women S. 338 3 years	I

77

Andorra	Legal	l
Angola	Illegal "Offence against public morality"	p
Antigua and Barbuda	Legal	l
Argentina	Not mentioned in law as such "offence against morality" punishable by 30 days	p
Armenia	Illegal for men	p
Aruba	Legal from 16 years	p
Australia	Legal (except Tasmania men-25 years)	a
Austria	Legal from age 18 since 1971	p
Azerbaijan	Illegal for men	p
Bahamas	Illegal for men and women S. 390 men S.52g women 10 years. (Law due to be repealed)	gl
Bahrain	Illegal for men and women Sharia Law applies	p
Bangladesh	Illegal for men and women Up to 7 years	p
Barbados	Illegal for men and women	p
Belarus	Legal since 1994	a
Belgium	Legal from age 16 since 1792	l
Belize	Legal since 1988	p
Benin	Not mentioned in law	l

Bermuda	Illegal for men S 173: homosexual act – 10 years attempted contact – 5 years	l
Bhutan	Illegal for men	l
Bolivia	Legal	l
Bosnia-Herzegovina	Illegal for men S. 93.2: "unnatural debauchery" 1 year	a
Botswana	Illegal for men S. 164a S. 167: "carnal knowledge against the order of nature" - 2 years	a
Brazil	Legal	l
Brunei	No legal information obtained	p
Bulgaria	Legal from age 21 since 1968	p
Burkino Faso	Legal from age 21 S. 331	l
Burundi	Not in law as such, but punishable as an "immoral act"	a
Cambodia	No legal information obtained	gl
Cameroon	Not mentioned in law as such	gl
Canada	Legal from age 18 since 1988	gl
Cape Verde	Illegal for men and women "Acts against nature" "Assaults on public or personal decency" S. 390 S.391 S.405 S.406	gl
Cayman Islands	Legal	gl

79

Central African Republic	Not mentioned in law as such	gl
Chad	Not mentioned in law as such	gl
Chile	Illegal for men Art 365 moves to decriminalise sodomy laws	gl
China	Legal Some prosecutions under S.106: "hooliganism", "disturbance against the social order" – 5 years	gl
Colombia	Legal	gl
Comoros	No information obtained	p
Congo	Legal	gl
Cook Islands	Illegal for men S. 206: buggery - 10 years S. 207: attempted buggery and indecent assault – 5 years	gl
Costa Rica	Legal from age 18	gl
Croatia	Legal from age 18	gl
Cuba	Illegal for men and women Art 303-9 "Public scandal" – 1 year	p
Cyprus	Legal since 1993	a
Czech Republic	Legal from age 15	gl
Denmark	Legal since 1930	gl
Djibouti	Illegal	a

Dominica	No information obtained	p
Dominican Republic	Legal but often punished as "offence against morality"	p
Ecuador	Illegal for men Art. 516 – up to 8 years	gl
Egypt	Not mentioned in law as such	p
El Salvador	Not mentioned in law as such	p
Equatorial Guinea	Not mentioned in law as such	p
Estonia	Legal since 1992	p
Ethiopia	Illegal for men and women S. 601 S.602 up to 3 years	p
Falklands	Legal as UK	gl
Fiji	Illegal for men S.168 : "Carnal knowledge against the order of nature" 14 years S. 169: attempts – 7 years S. 170: gross indecency – 5 years plus possible corporal punishment	l
Finland	Legal since 1971	p
France	Legal since 1791	l
French Guyana	Legal	l
French Polynesia	Legal	l
Gabon	Legal	l
Gambia	No information obtained	

Georgia	illegal for men Art. 121	I
Germany	Legal	I
Ghana	Illegal for men	I
Greece	Legal	I
Guinnea	No legal information available	p
Guinea Bissau	No legal information available	p
Grenada	No information obtained	
Guatamala	Legal	I
Guyana	Illegal for men S. 353 – possible life imprisonment S.242: buggery – 10 years S. 351: attempted buggery – 2 years	I
Haiti	Legal	I
Honduras	Legal	I
Hong Kong	Legal since 1991	I
Hungary	Legal since 1961	I
Iceland	Legal from age 14	
India	Illegal for men S. 377: "Unnatural act against the order of nature" – life, beating with lathi, or fine	I
Indonesia	Not mentioned in law as such	I
Iran	Illegal for men and women	I

	Sharia Articles 139 - 156 – execution including death by stoning, or cleaving in two; amputation of hands or feet, whipping	
Iraq	Not mentioned in law as such	gl
Ireland	Legal since 1993	a
Israel	Legal since 1988	l
Italy	Legal since 1889	l
Ivory Coast	Not mentioned in law as such	p
Jamaica	Illegal for men S. 76-9 – 10 years	gl
Jordan	Illegal for men	l
Kazakhstan	Legal since 1993	a
Kenya	Illegal for men S. 162 - 5: "carnal knowledge against the order of nature" – 14 years + corporal punishment	l
Kiribati	Illegal for men S.153 : buggery – 14 years S.155 : attempted buggery – 7 years S.155: gross indecency, private or public – 5 years	gl
Korea, Republic of	No information obtained	
Korea, Democratic Republic of	No information obtained	p
Kuwait	Illegal for men and women Sharia Laws apply	gl

Kyrgystan	Illegal for men and women Art. 112	a
Laos	No information obtained. (Arrests of homosexuals reported 1992)	
Latvia	Legal since 1992	a
Lebanon	Illegal for men and women	p
Lesotho	Not mentioned in law	l
Liberia	Not mentioned in law	l
Libya	Illegal for men and women Section 407 (4) – 5 years	l
Lithuania	Legal since 1993	l
Luxembourg	Legal since 1792 from age 16	l
Macau	Legal	l
Macedonia	Illegal for men S.101 (2) – 1 year	l
Madagascar	Not mentioned in law	p
Malawi	Illegal for men and women Art. 153: "unnatural offences" Art. 156: Public decency	l
Malaysia	Illegal for men. S 377 - 20 years, fine, whipping gross male indecency – 2 years	l
Maldives	Illegal for men	l
Mali	Illegal	l

Malta	Legal from age 18 since 1973	p
Martinique	Legal	gl
Mauritania	Illegal for men and women Sharia laws apply – execution	gl
Mexico	Legal	gl
Moldova	Illegal for men	gl
Monaco	Legal	gl
Mongolia	No information obtained	a
Montenegro	Legal from 14 since 1977	gl
Morocco	Illegal for men and women "Unnatural sex" liable to prosecution S489 – 3 years, 1000 dinar fine	gl
Mozambique	Illegal for men and women S. 70, 71 – 3 years	gl
Namibia	illegal for men and women "unnatural sex acts" liable to prosecution	gl
Nauru	No information obtained	p
Netherlands	Legal since 1811 from 16	p
Netherlands Antilles	Legal from 16	l
New Zealand	Legal from age 16	p
New Caledonia	Legal	p
Nigeria	Illegal for men "carnal knowledge against the order of nature" Art. 214 – 14 years	gl

Niuwe	Illegal for men S 170 buggery 10 years S. 171 indecent assaults on men – 5 years	gl
Norway	Legal from age 17 since 1972	p
Oman	Illegal for men and women S.32 – 3 years	p
Pakistan	Illegal for men and women "carnal knowledge against the order of nature" S.377 - life + 100 lashes	p
Panama	Legal	p
Papua New Guinea	Illegal for men	p
Paraguay	Not mentioned in law	p
Peru	Legal except Police and Military	gl
Philippines	Legal	gl
Poland	Legal since 1969	gl
Portugal	Legal from age	gl
Qatar	Illegal. Sharia Law applies	p
Reunion	Legal	gl
Romania	Illegal "if causing public scandal" Art. 200 – 5 years	a
Russian Federation	Legal from age 15 since 1993	a
Rwanda	Not mentioned in law	gl
St Lucia	Illegal for men and women	p

Samoa, Western	Illegal for men and women 58S – 7 years	p
San Marino	Illegal for men and women "if causing public scandal" Art. 274 – possible imprisonment	p
Saudi Arabia	Illegal for men and women Sharia law applies – Execution	p
Senegal	illegal for men and women – fines	p
Seychelles	Illegal for men and women	p
Sierra Leone	illegal: "unnatural act"	h
Singapore	Illegal for men and women S.377: "carnal intercourse against the order of nature" – life S. 377a: gross indecency - 2 years	gl
Slovakia	Legal from age 15	gl
Slovenia	Legal from age 14	gl
Somalia	Illegal. Art 409 – 3 years	a
Solomon Islands	Illegal for men S. 153 buggery – 14 years S. 154 attempted buggery – 7 years	gl
South Africa	Legal from age 19 since 1994	a
Spain	Legal from 1822	gl
Sri Lanka	Illegal for men S 365 – 10 years	gl
Sudan	Illegal.	gl

	Sharia Law applies – execution	
Surinam	Legal from age 18	gl
Swaziland	Illegal for men and women – prison or fine	gl
Sweden	Legal from age 15	gl
Switzerland	Legal since 1942	gl
Syria	Illegal for men and women S.52 "carnal knowledge against the order of nature – 3 years"	gl
Taiwan	Legal for men and women. Offence for soldiers "converted to homosexuality" – possible execution	gl
Tanzania	Illegal for men Art. 154-7 – 14 years	gl
Thailand	Legal from age 16	gl
Togo	Illegal for men – 3 years	p
Tonga	Illegal for men S.126: "the abominable crime of sodomy" – life S.127 attempts – 7 years	gl
Trinidad	Illegal for men and women S.13: Sexual Offences Act: buggery – 10 years S 16 serious indecency – 2 years	gl
Tunisia	Illegal for men and women and women S. 230	gl
Turkey	Legal. Prosecutions under indecency laws.	gl

Turkmenistan	Illegal S.126 5 years	gl
Uganda	Illegal for men S 140 "carnal knowledge against the order of nature" – life S.141 attempts - 7 years S.143: procurement or gross indecency – 5 years	gl
Ukraine	Legal since 1991	a
United Arab Emirates	Illegal for men and women "unnatural offences" – 14 years "obscene acts" – fine or 2 years	p
United Kingdom	Legal from age 18	gl
United States	Legal in most states except Arkansas, Kansas, Missouri, Montana, Tennessee	gl
Uruguay	Legal	gl
Uzbekistan	Illegal for men Art 100	gl
Vanuatu	Legal	gl
Vatican City	Legal	gl
Venezuela	Legal from age 18	gl
Vietnam	Not mentioned in law	p
Yemen	Illegal for men and women – Sharia laws apply	p
Zaire	Illegal for men and women S. 168-172: "crime against family life"	p

Zambia	Illegal for men: S 155-8 – 14 years	p
Zimbabwe	illegal for men – fines	p

AMNESTY INTERNATIONAL NEEDS YOUR HELP

Since Amnesty International began to take up cases of lesbian and gay men as prisoners of conscience, it has been in touch with a growing number of organisations working for homosexual equality round the world. Amnesty International recognises the struggle for gay and lesbian human rights as one aspect of the struggle to ensure all rights for all people.

Amnesty International considers for adoption anyone who is imprisoned

- safely because of their homosexuality, including the practice of homosexual acts in private between consenting adults
- for advocating homosexual equality;
- on charges of homosexuality when these have been used as a pretext and the real reason for their imprisonment is the expression of their political, religious or other conscientiously-held beliefs.

Furthermore, Amnesty International opposes the torture and execution of anyone, including those tortured and killed for their real or perceived homosexuality.

Amnesty International is interested in receiving further information on violations of the rights of gay men and lesbians that may be taking place anywhere in the world. Information would be welcomed in the form of written reports, witness statements, articles, press cuttings, film clips, photos, and so on.

If you, or someone you know has fallen victim to such a violation, please send a detailed letter describing the abuse to:

Amnesty International
International Secretariat
1 Easton Street
London WCIX 8DJ
United Kingdom

Phone 0171 413 5500
FAX   0171 956 1157

FILM

"Breaking the Silence" is the title of a hard-hitting 22 minute film in colour about homosexual repression in many countries, including a number of the examples quoted in this book. It shows the work of some of those organising to defend the rights of lesbians and gay men. The video was made for Amnesty International Netherlands by Shirley Armstrong in 1995. It can be borrowed from the AIUK GLBT Network, AIUK Section Office, on the provison that it is to be shown only to non-paying audiences, and is not for broadcasting. It is available for a cost of £5 to cover post and packaging. UK PAL format only.